TWAYNE'S WORLD AUTHORS SERIES
A Survey of the World's Literature

SPAIN

Janet W. Díaz, Texas Tech University

EDITOR

Azorín
(José Martínez Ruiz)

TWAS 604

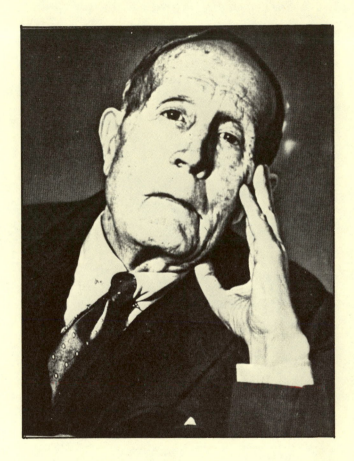

Azorín
(José Martínez Ruiz)

AZORÍN
(JOSÉ MARTÍNEZ RUIZ)

By KATHLEEN M. GLENN
Wake Forest University

TWAYNE PUBLISHERS
A DIVISION OF G. K. HALL & CO., BOSTON

Published in 1981 by Twayne Publishers,
A Division of G. K. Hall & Co.

Printed on permanent/durable acid-free paper and bound
in the United States of America

First Printing

Frontispiece photo of Azorín courtesy of Ediciones Destino

Library of Congress Cataloging in Publication Data

Glenn, Kathleen Mary.
Azorín (José Martínez Ruiz)

(Twayne's world authors series ; TWAS 604 : Spain)
Bibliography: p. 156–58
Includes index.
1. Martínez Ruiz, José, 1873-1967—Criticism and Interpretation.
PQ6623.A816Z597   868'.62'09   80-23267
ISBN 0-8057-6446-1

To Kathryn

Contents

About the Author

Preface

Chronology

1. Introduction   13

2. Years of Apprenticeship   25

3. Success and Maturity: I. Novels   37

4. Success and Maturity: II. Essays and Sketches   65

5. New Experiments   94

6. A Time for Recapitulation   114

7. Conclusion   135

   Notes and References   139

   Selected Bibliography   156

   Index   159

About the Author

Kathleen M. Glenn is Associate Professor of Spanish at Wake Forest University and has also taught at the University of Santa Clara and at Kansas State University since receiving her doctorate from Stanford University in 1970. She is an associate editor of *Anales de la Narrativa Española Contemporánea* and a member of the editorial board of the *Journal of Spanish Studies: Twentieth Century* and the *Annual Bibliography of Post–Civil War Spanish Fiction*. She is also a member of the advisory board of the Society of Spanish and Spanish-American Studies.

Professor Glenn is the author of *The Novelistic Technique of Azorín* (1973) and has contributed articles and reviews to such journals as *Anales de la Narrativa Española Contemporánea, Estudos Ibero-Americanos, Hispanófila, Quaderni Ibero-Americani, Revista de Estudios Hispánicos, Romance Notes, American Hispanist,* and *Modern Language Journal.*

Preface

Although José Martínez Ruiz (Azorín) was one of the central figures of the Generation of 1898 and a major twentieth-century author, he is not widely known by English readers. In introducing him to those who are not specialists in Spanish literature, I have sought to give a representative picture of his work. Its sheer volume—recent bibliographies list some 140 titles—and the limited space here available preclude a comprehensive analysis. I have chosen for special attention those of his books which are most significant, either because of their artistic merit or because of the light they shed on Azorín's intellectual development. Because of the fundamental unity of his literary production and the extent to which it revolves around certain lasting preoccupations, an illustration of its essential characteristics does not require a review of everything Azorín ever wrote. Thus the body of the present text is selective in focus, as are the Chronology and the Bibliography. This last section, in particular, is intended as a guide to the general reader who wishes to expand his knowledge of Azorín.

I have concentrated on the novels and most important collections of sketches and essays and have given minimal consideration to Azorín's short stories and plays. For the benefit of the reader who may be unfamiliar with the novels, I have summarized their contents in some detail before discussing the interrelationship of theme and form. My critical approach has been eclectic: besides attempting a brief outline of the history of ideas and events during the period of Azorín's activity, I have tried to analyze his texts closely for both meaning and technique. I have utilized the methods which seemed most appropriate to the works in question and most likely to contribute to a fuller understanding and appreciation of them. When relevant, supplementary biographical information has also been included. With respect to Azorín's literary criticism, I have presented his critical theory and given an overview of his essays on Spanish literature before proceeding to a perusal of his four major collections of essays. Through liberal paraphrasing of the original Spanish texts I have tried to convey at least some idea of the flavor of Azorín's style, a flavor which is virtually impossible to capture in translation.

Following a brief biographical study and a preliminary discussion of Azorín's obsession with time, Chapter 2 deals with his years of apprenticeship. Chapters 3 and 4 are devoted to his best-known works, the novels and volumes of essays and sketches published between 1902 and 1925. Chapter 5 focuses on his period of most intensive experimentation, 1926–1931, and Chapter 6 on his last novels and volumes of memoirs. A short bibliography lists Azorín's principal books and the most useful critical studies of his work. The notes contain references to many additional studies of a more specialized nature. Throughout the text I have used the name Azorín, for it is under this pseudonym that Martínez Ruiz is known.

I wish to acknowledge my indebtedness to Professor Bernard Gicovate of Stanford University and to express my deep appreciation of his painstaking reading of the manuscript. His help and advice have been invaluable. I should like to thank Wake Forest University for its generosity, both in the form of grants from its Research and Publication Fund and the leave which enabled me to complete this book.

Chronology

1873　June 8: born in Monóvar, Spain.
1878　First schooling in Monóvar.
1880　Begins studies in Piarist school in Yecla.
1888　Enrolls in the University of Valencia as a law student.
1893–　Publishes first literary criticism and sociopolitical works.
1896　Moves to Madrid in 1896.
1897–　Additional satirical and expository works, plus a collection
1899　of short stories. Spanish-American War of 1898.
1900　*El alma castellana (1600-1800).*
1901　*Diario de un enfermo.* Pilgrimage to Larra's grave.
1902　*La voluntad.*
1903　*Antonio Azorín.*
1904　Contributes to *España. Las confesiones de un pequeño filósofo.*
1905　*Los pueblos* (first book published under pen name Azorín). Contributes to *El Imparcial* before joining staff of *ABC. La ruta de Don Quijote.*
1907　Serves first of five terms in Parliament.
1908　Marries Julia Guinda Urzanqui.
1909　*España.*
1912　*Lecturas españolas* and *Castilla.*
1913　*Clásicos y modernos.*
1914　*Los valores literarios.*
1915　*Al margen de los clásicos* and *El licenciado Vidriera visto por Azorín* (later titled *Tomás Rueda*).
1916　Begins contributing to *La Prensa* of Buenos Aires.
1917–　Serves briefly as Undersecretary of Education.
1918
1922　*Don Juan.*
1924　Election to Real Academia Española and publication of his acceptance address, *Una hora de España (Entre 1560 y 1590).*

1925 *Doña Inés.*
1928 *Félix Vargas* (later titled *El caballero inactual*).
1929 *Superrealismo* (later titled *El libro de Levante*).
1930 *Pueblo.*
1931 Proclamation of Second Republic.
1936– Resides in Paris during Spanish Civil War, returning to
1939   Madrid in August 1939.
1942 *El escritor.*
1943 *El enfermo* and *Capricho.*
1944 Publication of *La isla sin aurora, María Fontán, Salvadora de Olbena,* and the first of a series of collections of articles.
1946 *Memorias inmemoriales.*
1947– Publication of *Obras completas.*
1954
1967 March 2: dies in Madrid.

CHAPTER 1

Introduction

IN recounting the early experiences of the protagonist of one of his novels, Azorín has depicted the puzzlement and wonder which marked his own childhood and has expressed one of the preoccupations which defines him as a writer—the effort to recapture moments of his personal past as well as the past of his tradition and his country. In *Tomás Rueda* he has fused autobiographical and literary elements, portraying himself while giving new life to a character invented 300 years earlier by Cervantes. Azorín first describes the child Tomás standing at an attic window and gazing out over the rooftops of a Castilian city. On the lower floors of the house people bustle about, but the sounds of their movements are barely audible in the quiet, dimly lit attic filled with discarded furniture and old books. The pensive, melancholy child is clearly "at home" in a world of silence and solitude. A second, distant window which is inexplicably illuminated and then darkened in the night disturbs the boy, and as an adult he continues to puzzle over the mystery of it. Standing outside a third window Tomás observes a traveling actor who has amused the townspeople with his antics. Now that the performance is over, the ailing actor gives way to his private grief and concern for what will become of his family after his death. Years later when the adult Tomás looks back on this last scene he comprehends that the third window was a mirror in which he saw his own image reflected, that of "the man who laughs and suffers."[1]

The anguished perception of the effects of the passage of time and the contrast between outward appearance and inner reality— visible in the figure of the actor—are salient features of Azorín's writing. He, like Tomás, is essentially a contemplative individual, a spectator of the lives of others, elevated above and somewhat detached from the rest of the world, as in the attic setting, or on the outside looking in, as in the case of the third window, or gazing into the distance trying to decipher impenetrable mysteries. And he is constantly attuned to the reverberations of the past.

Many of Azorín's works provide information about certain aspects of his life. Several of the volumes of memoirs which were written in the 1940s are particularly rich in detail. The following pages incorporate much of this autobiographical material. It is, however, necessary to recognize that Azorín's memoirs are not always a reliable source. There are several reasons for the inaccuracy or falseness of autobiographical narratives.[2] One is that we forget, and this forgetfulness becomes more pronounced with age. While some errors or deletions thus are attributable to lapses of memory, others are due to the deliberate censorship exercised by the mind upon that which is disagreeable or embarrassing. And human beings are inclined to rationalize their actions and to present them in the most favorable light possible. These reasons help explain the inconsistencies found in Azorín's accounts of his life. The views of the elderly archconservative differ in many ways from those of the fiery young anarchist of the 1890s. The nostalgia of old age also leads to a mellowing of the anger and bitterness of youth, as is evident in the contrasting versions which Azorín offers of his early schooling. By correlating his testimony with that of his main biographers, we shall attempt to differentiate between facts and fiction, even though Azorín, like many of the protagonists of his later works, probably would have maintained that it is impossible to do so.

I Monóvar, Yecla, and Valencia

Monóvar, situated in the valley of Elda in the province of Alicante, was in the nineteenth century a prosperous, quiet town. There José Augusto Trinidad Martínez Ruiz was born on June 8, 1873, the first of the nine children of Isidro Martínez and María Luisa Ruiz. Don Isidro, a native of Yecla, was comfortably well-off and, although he had a law degree, devoted himself to caring for his properties and serving as conservative mayor of Monóvar. Azorín was never particularly close to his father. In contrast, he repeatedly mentions his mother and affectionately remembers her as a tender, sensitive woman of natural elegance. In his *Memorias inmemoriales* (Memories of Time Immemorial) he speaks of the decisive influence a mother has upon her child. He seems to attribute to Doña María's example his own sense of order and meticulousness, suggesting that her desire that everything be neat and in its proper place affected his prose style. His mother was in the habit of jotting down all the daily events of the family's life, and she carefully recorded household expenditures. This attention to detail and to the commonplace is also found in her son's writing.

At the age of five Pepe, as the boy was called, began attending the local school, and his experiences there are described in *Las confesiones de un pequeño filósofo* (The Confessions of a Little Philosopher). He recollects, with considerable distaste, the garish lithographs which adorned the schoolroom walls and the fact that after the other students were dismissed for the day he was forced to remain behind for the special lessons he was "privileged" to receive as a son of the mayor. These lessons usually ended with Pepe breaking into sobs and the teacher shaking his head in dismay and wondering what on earth was wrong with the boy. The image which emerges from *The Confessions* is that of a serious child who spends his days slaving over his primers and struggling to learn to read.

When he was seven he was sent to a school in Yecla which was run by the Piarist teaching order. In *The Confessions* he recalls becoming "sadder than ever" (II, 44) with the arrival of autumn and the prospect of suddenly being torn away from the delightful paradise of his hometown and being buried in the gloomy cavern of Yecla. One year in a futile attempt to escape he leapt from the cart which was bearing him toward his father's birthplace and dashed across the fields, only to be caught and borne inexorably onward.

The years spent in Yecla left a deep impression upon Azorín. He has portrayed the city as a depressing, joyless place of somber colors and harsh climate where the predominant sound was the ringing of church bells calling the inhabitants to mass or tolling for the dead. The prevailing mentality was one of resignation, summed up in the oft-repeated "What can we do?", "His time had come" (said of the dead), and "It is already [too] late." Azorín ascribes to that last phrase the beginning of his obsession with the relentless passage of time. The routine at the school was as severe and deadening as the city itself: mass every morning, prayers twice daily, five hours of class, four and one-half hours of study, and only two of play. There were but few bright spots, one being the mealtime reading of selections from Jules Verne or from *Don*

Quixote, and another the excursions to gather insects for classification. And yet, in 1941 Azorín wrote of the years spent with the Piarists as the best of his life, saying that they instilled in him a sense of seriousness and a concern for things of the spirit (IX, 1221). The mature writer, alternately drawn to the sensuous and the spiritual, saw his sensibility as a product of the dual influence of Monóvar, Mediterranean or Levantine in character, and of Yecla, Manchegan or Castilian.

In the fall of 1888 Azorín enrolled in the University of Valencia, planning to study law. In general, he was not a good student, and he failed a course in Spanish literature. Rather than preparing for his classes he preferred to spend his time reading in the university library, attending the theater and the bullfights, browsing through secondhand bookstores, or taking long walks around the city and the neighboring countryside. Valencia, unlike Monóvar or Yecla, was an active, bustling provincial capital where political issues were hotly debated. There he began his career as a journalist, and in 1894 and 1895 he contributed to *El Mercantil Valenciano*, *Bellas Artes*, and the radical paper *El Pueblo*. It was during the years spent in Valencia that he, like many in late-nineteenth-century Europe, became attracted to the anarchist dream of an ideal society in which all forms of coercive control and authority would be abolished, enabling men to coexist in fraternal love and freedom. In a number of his early works he espoused anarchist ideas, proclaiming that those institutions—the State, the Church, marriage—which limit the freedom of the individual should be done away with.

II   *The Generation of 1898 and Madrid*

In 1896 Azorín abandoned his law studies and set off for Madrid, determined to win a name for himself in the literary world. The works he published during his early years in the capital contain numerous references to the frustrations of that period: financial problems to which he was unaccustomed, the difficulty of gaining entry to major journals, and the friction between established men of letters and young writers who were still struggling to win renown. There was, however, a degree of camaraderie among the aspiring authors. They tended to frequent the same *tertulias* or literary gatherings, published in the same newspapers, and contributed to various shortlived literary magazines, such as *Revista Nueva*, *Arte Joven*, and *Juventud*.

The young writers who later would be known as the Generation of 1898 shared certain concerns. In various articles published between 1910 and 1913 Azorín sketched a profile of his generation, which included Pío Baroja, Ramiro de Maeztu, Miguel de Unamuno, Ramón María del Valle-Inclán, Jacinto Benavente, and Antonio Machado.[3] In Azorín's opinion, these authors were characterized by their profound love of art, their spirit of protest against existing formulae, their independence, and their idealism. They represented the continuation of a current of social and political criticism which dated back to at least the seventeenth century. The spectacle of the *desastre* (Spain's defeat in the Spanish-American War) intensified the already existing discontent and the conviction that a radical change in Spanish life was essential. The *noventayochistas* (the writers of the Generation of 1898) perceived the need for greater attention to reality, increased familiarity with the philosophical and scientific ideas being discussed in other countries, and a knowledge of Spain's own history and art. In literature they represented a rebirth in which national thought was nourished by ideas from abroad.[4] And lastly, writes Azorín, the Generation loved the old towns and countryside of Spain, revered primitive poets (Gonzalo de Berceo, Juan Ruiz, the Marqués de Santillana) and the painter El Greco, rehabilitated the seventeenth-century poet Luis de Góngora, and felt enthusiasm for Mariano José de Larra, the leading figure of Spanish Romanticism.

Reacting against the hollowness, superficiality, and facile optimism of the time, the members of the Generation examined with a critical eye all aspects of Spanish life—political, social, economic, religious, intellectual, and artistic. They studied the past in an attempt to find the roots of present problems and possible solutions for the future. Behind their sweeping criticism of the Spain they knew lay the dream of an ideal Spain. The phrase *amor amargo* (bitter love) aptly sums up their feeling for their country.[5] They searched for the "real" Spain in the countryside and the *pueblo* (common people). Although they were not Castilian by birth, it was in the old towns and barren plains of Castile that they found the essence of Spain. Emotion colored their vision of the landscape. Between the eye of the beholder and what was beheld there was interposed an image of the Spain of the past and a dream of the Spain of the future.[6] Their veneration for medieval writers was a result not only of their rejection of the rhetorical, declamatory literature of the second half of the nineteenth century but also of their view of the Middle Ages as a more authentic period. Despite their shared preoccupations, the members of the group were men of marked individualism.

What was to be a lifelong friendship developed between two of the *noventayochistas*, Baroja and Azorín. They visited Toledo in 1900 and were sufficiently impressed by the nocturnal scene of a child's coffin being carried through the city's streets to relate the incident in several of their novels, Baroja in *Camino de perfección* (The Way to Perfection) and Azorín in *Diario de un enfermo* (Diary of a Sick Man) and *La voluntad* (Will).[7] Along with Maeztu they formed the Group of Three and issued various protests against sociopolitical inequities, calling for concrete proposals to deal with the problems of Spain. In 1902 Azorín helped organize a banquet in honor of the publication of Baroja's *The Way to Perfection*. One of the most significant acts of these early years was the 1901 visit to the Madrid cemetery where Larra, their Romantic predecessor, was buried. There Azorín read a speech praising Larra as an idealist tormented by the same anguish as those now paying homage to him.[8] They, he declared, venerate him as a master and identify with his personal characteristics—the sincerity, the impetuosity, the passion, and the skepticism that drove him to suicide—and with his attempts to revitalize the Spanish language.

By 1904 Azorín had contributed to some thirty different newspapers and magazines, many of which were of limited circulation.[9] That year he became a reporter for the newspaper *España*, writing a series of rather irreverent "Parliamentary Impressions" in which he satirized the pomposity and posturing of the congressmen, most of whom inspired little respect. The following year he achieved his ambition of writing for the prestigious paper *El Imparcial*, but this success was brief indeed. Several indiscreet pieces about a prominent politician and a series of strongly worded articles on the situation in Andalusia, where a severe drought and the destruction of vineyards by phylloxera had led to widespread unemployment, resulted in his being dismissed from the paper. He then joined the staff of the conservative *ABC*.

Azorín had now arrived in the literary world and had to his credit five important books: the novels *Will* (1902), *Antonio Azorín* (1903), and *The Confessions of a Little Philosopher* (1904), plus *Los pueblos* (Towns, 1905) and *La ruta de Don Quijote* (The Route of Don Quixote, 1905), these last two being collections of articles which had appeared in *España* and *El Imparcial*. In writing the 1902–1904 novels about Antonio Azorín, his literary alter ego, Azorín had resolved the question of whether he should pursue an active or a reflective existence, and in so doing he had "created" a new self.[10] The change from anarchist to "little philosopher" is symbolized in the adoption of his definitive pen name, Azorín.[11] Previously his works had appeared under a variety of names. He had used the pseudonyms Cándido (an allusion to Voltaire's Candide) in 1893 and Ahrimán (the spirit of evil in Zoroastrianism) in 1894. The books published between 1895 and 1904 had appeared under his legal name, J. Martínez Ruiz. In 1904 he began using the pen name Azorín for his newspaper articles, and from 1905 on all his works appeared under this name.

Azorín's new intellectual and artistic orientation is paralleled by a growing political conservatism. In 1907 Unamuno reproached him for having abandoned his former ardor as a critic of society and suggested that Martínez Ruiz, the outspoken rebel, had become a prisoner of Azorín, the little philosopher, and that the latter should be told to "go take a walk."[12] That same year Azorín descended from the press gallery to the floor of the Parliament and served the first of five terms as a congressman, representing Purchena in 1907, Puenteareas in 1914, and Sorbas in 1916, 1918, and 1919. He also briefly held the post of Undersecretary of Education in 1917–1918 and in 1919. He first entered Parliament under the aegis of the conservative leader Antonio Maura.[13] The fact that Azorín, mordant critic of politics and politicians, would serve in Parliament was bad enough, but that he should do so under the conservative banner scandalized many of his colleagues. His political about-face apparently was the result of his having relinquished his early dreams of sweeping changes in Spanish society and his having decided that a policy of gradual modifications and small reforms imposed from above was more practical. Joining the conservatives did not mean that he had ceased to be a critic of Spain.

One more important change in his views takes place in 1908 when the former critic of the institution of marriage and advocate of free love married. Julia Guinda Urzanqui, in many ways like Azorín's mother, was the ideal companion for him. Her optimism and warmth provided a counterbalance to his pessimism and aloofness. On several occasions Azorín paid tribute to his wife's spontaneity and eternal youthfulness. In *Memories* he confessed that he did not know what would have become of him without her. Referring to himself as X he wrote: "X is retiring, and Julia communicative. X frequently lives in a future which he expects to be ill-fated, and Julia lives in a present filled with hope" (VIII, 397). During the years of their marriage she was his constant support. Thus, by 1908, the pattern of Azorín's life was set: a placid home life, a secure position with *ABC*, occasional ventures into public affairs, and the time to write a steady stream of articles and books.

The Spanish Civil War (1936-1939) abruptly ended this peaceful existence. In October 1930 Azorín had left *ABC*, and from then until the summer of 1936 he had written for a series of less conservative newspapers.[14] Shortly before the advent of the Second Republic in 1931, he had declared himself a Republican and in favor of an end to the long rule of Hapsburg and Bourbon monarchs who, in his view, had diverted Spain from its true tradition of federalism. In the articles he wrote during the first months of the Republic there is a resurgence of the combative spirit of his youth, as he defends the new government and warns of the dangers which face it. This initial enthusiasm soon waned, and several months after the strong showing of the Right and Center parties in the April 1933 municipal elections he announced the end of his "militant journalism."

After the outbreak of the Civil War, Azorín and his wife moved to Paris, where they subsisted on the income derived from the articles and short stories he sent to *La Prensa* of Buenos Aires. Even more distressing than the economic problems of the war years was Azorín's uncertainty as to whether he would ever be able to return to his beloved Spain. His days in Paris followed the same general pattern as they had in Madrid. He read, wrote, spent hours in the Louvre and the bookstalls along the Seine, and visited with other émigrés, but the cornerstone of his life—Spain—was missing. The profound emotional impact of his exile is apparent in the short stories he wrote during these years. The titles of the volumes in which many of these stories were collected reflect his obsession with his homeland: *Españoles en París* (Spaniards in Paris), *Pensando en España* (Thinking about Spain), and *Sintiendo a España* (Feeling Spain or, less literally, My Feelings for Spain). In the first of these collections, in particular, the mask of impassivity which Azorín often assumed is stripped away, and the intensity of his anguish is laid bare. A sensation of aching loss pervades the book, and the word *dolor* (pain, grief) appears again and again. In one sketch he alludes to his feeling of disorientation, describing himself as physically present in Paris but in Madrid in spirit, and he wonders what is happening in the Spanish capital, what has become of relatives left behind.

In many of the stories compiled in *Thinking about Spain* and *Feeling Spain* Azorín evokes the literary and historical past of his country, spinning fantasies about Cervantes and several of his most famous characters, Don Juan de Austria (half-brother of Philip II), and Roderick (the Visigothic king who, according to legend, was responsible for the fall of Spain to the Moors in 711). The remembrance of things past serves as a consolation and as a refuge from the harsh reality of the present. The protagonists of a number of tales are aging authors and painters—Azorín was now in his sixties— who have spent their lives portraying Spain and who, in exile, have come to see their native land with great clarity. One of these painters declares that no one has surpassed him in his love for the people, landscapes, towns, literature, and history of Spain, the subjects about which Azorín had been writing for more than forty years.

After returning to Madrid in August 1939, he began work on the first of four volumes of memoirs and gradually picked up the thread of his prewar life.[15] In 1941 he resumed writing for *ABC* and between 1942 and 1944, in a burst of productivity, he published six novels.[16] Although he announced in 1952 that he planned to retire, he continued writing until shortly before his death in 1967. During the post-Civil War years he led an increasingly reclusive existence, preoccupied with his health and fearful of emotional disturbances, withdrawn from the external world, receiving few visitors. Most of the companions of his youth were in exile or dead, and his friend Baroja died in 1956. In his last years Azorín's financial position was secure, for the Premio March which he was awarded in 1958 brought him the sum of 500,000 pesetas. During his lifetime he had been accorded many tributes and in 1924 he had been elected to membership in the Royal Spanish Academy. The government had also bestowed upon him the Great Cross of Alphonso the Wise and that of Isabella the Catholic. But by the time of his death on March 2, 1967, at the age of ninety-three, Azorín held little interest for the socially oriented writers of the day, and the 1973 centenary of his birth passed with comparatively little fanfare, a fact which must have saddened his widow, who died on January 17, 1974, at the age of ninety-eight. All too often, non-literary factors have colored ap-

praisals of Azorín's writing, and anger over his political conservatism has led some critics to dismiss him as passé. This assessment,
however, ignores how much he has contributed to twentieth-
century literature and to the understanding and appreciation of the
cultural heritage of Spain.

III   *Time and Literature*

Azorín's concern with time helps explain some of the distinctive
features of his works. Subject matter, tempo, choice of tenses, language, and—in the case of his novels, in particular—structure are
affected by this obsession. Looking about him the young Azorín is
painfully aware of evanescence and destruction, of "the inexorable
course of all our being and of the things that surround us toward the
mysterious ocean of Nothingness" (I, 898). He feels the present
constantly slipping away from him. As a writer he attempts to
counteract the effects of the flight of time by presenting a series of
arrested moments, by turning to the concept of eternal recurrence,
and by creating the illusion of timelessness. Ultimately he declares
that the distinction between past, present, and future is invalid,
that there is only one plane of time: an eternal present.[17]

The artist, by immobilizing a fleeting moment, can fix and thus
eternalize that moment. In *Madrid* Azorín states that the writers of
the Generation of 1898 gave new aesthetic form to sensations. Influenced by El Greco's use of discordantly contrasted colors, Góngora's
presentation of isolated sensations, and the painting of the Impressionists, they sought to present pure sensations. The fragmentary
and static nature of Azorín's novels, the predominance of the
present and present perfect tenses, and the concentration upon the
small occurrences (*menudos hechos*) which "form the subtle fabric
of daily life" (VI, 232) are, at least in part, the result of his attempt
to reproduce sensation and stop time, to give enduring form to the
fleeting moment.[18] His novels are constructed of a series of very
short, tenuously connected chapters, in each of which a fragment of
time is caught and preserved for eternity.[19] It is possible for Azorín
to use a deliberately discontinuous pattern of independent structural units because each unit is of comparable importance.[20] In his
novels there is almost no rise and fall in the action, which is minimal, no tightly constructed plot. Plot, he affirms, has nothing to do
with art. "Art is the capturing and gradation of nuances" (VII, 41)
and these nuances can be best presented in a static series of vi-

gnettes. A further advantage gained by presenting discrete moments is that Azorín thus avoids reproducing within the novel the temporal flow of the external world. A well-knit, fast-moving story would sweep the reader along from chapter to chapter in a headlong rush which would parallel the very flux Azorín is trying to resist.

As already noted, he believes that everyday life is composed of a delicate web of *menudos hechos*, and it is precisely everyday life which is preserved in the self-contained pictures which are his specialty. One of the criticisms which he levels against the theater is that the characters of most plays move in an atmosphere of abnormality, inasmuch as dramatists present adventures, extraordinary happenings. This is exactly the opposite of what Azorín does. Seemingly trivial details, ordinary incidents, and prosaic lives, these are what assume importance for him. They are all part of "the eternal poetry" (II, 543) of daily existence. But they are more than poetic; they are also enduring. The commonplace, that which is generically human, is endlessly repeated, while that which is unique or exceptional vanishes. *Los grandes hechos* (great occurrences) disappear into oblivion, but *los menudos hechos* persist.[21] Azorín points out that, in contrast to their predecessors, the writers of the Generation of 1898 adopt the aesthetic of the "beauties of the commonplace" (*primores de lo vulgar*),[22] focusing on what previous historians, novelists, and poets had considered unworthy of attention, and thereby incorporate in their work a rich vein of new material (VI, 232-33).

Azorín's obsession with time also explains his interest in the concept of eternal recurrence, which is frequently mentioned in the books published between 1902 and 1925. The unending repetition of certain basic human emotions and experiences provides for a type of permanence and continuity, as is demonstrated in several of the sketches in *Castilla* (Castile, 1912). The most famous of these is "Las nubes" (The Clouds), in which Azorín imagines that two famous lovers of Spanish literature, Calixto and Melibea of the *Celestina*, did not meet with a tragic death. In his version of their story, eighteen years have passed since Calixto first entered Melibea's garden in pursuit of a falcon. Now married, he appears to have everything a man could desire, and yet he sits quietly watching the clouds float by. These clouds are a visible manifestation of both temporality and eternity:

Contemplating them we sense how our being and all things race toward
nothingness, while they—so fleeting—remain eternal. These clouds which
we now contemplate were contemplated 200, 500, 1000, 3000 years ago by
other men with the same passions and the same longings as we. . . . To
live. . . is to see everything return—anguish, joys, hopes—like those clouds
which are always different and always the same, like those transitory and
immutable clouds. (II, 708-709)

As Calixto watches, history repeats itself. A young man enters the
garden—chasing a falcon—sees Calixto's daughter, smiles, and begins to speak to her.

External details will vary, but the substance of the scene will be
continually repeated. This idea is beautifully developed in "Una
ciudad y un balcón" (A City and a Balcony). The epigraph for the
sketch is a fragment from the sixteenth-century poèt Garcilaso de la
Vega: "No me podrán quitar el dolorido / Sentir" (No one can ever
deprive me of my sorrow). Azorín here observes a Castilian city in
three different moments. It is first seen around 1500, when a
woolens mill and various tanneries line the banks of the river. On a
balcony overlooking the city square there sits a man whose eyes "are
veiled by a profound sadness" (II, 692–93). Three centuries later
only one or two tanneries remain and the chants of the wool carders
are no longer heard in the city, but on the balcony in the square
there sits a man whose eyes "are veiled by a profound, indefinable
sadness" (II, 694). Later still, when the river is lined with factories,
on the balcony a man meditates. "An intense sadness dims his eyes"
(II, 696). Azorín portrays for us three very different worlds inhabited by three different men, each of whom feels the same emotion.
Despite the external changes, the essential experience remains unchanged, just as the final paragraph of each of the three main
sections of the sketch is basically the same despite variations in
wording.[23]

The principle that unchanging essence is manifested in ever-
changing form could stand as a description of Azorín's career as a
novelist. Over a period of forty-five years he reflected on the possibilities of the genre of the novel and experimented with different
techniques, all the while focusing on a limited number of fundamental preoccupations.

CHAPTER 2

Years of Apprenticeship

IN many cases the literary merit of Azorín's juvenilia is minimal, but the works he published during the closing years of the nineteenth century are of interest to us because of what they reveal about his personality and early intellectual development. The elderly Azorín described these works as "youthful peccadillos" (I, x) which were the product of a hodgepodge of readings, the fevered spirit of the times, and the intemperance natural to youth. He acknowledged that he had assailed "institutions and persons, events and things worthy of respect, admiration, and love" (I, x), mistakenly believing that they were Manchegan windmills concealing giants.

Alternating between literary criticism and sociopolitical studies, the youthful Azorín is a gadfly, attacking the literary world and existing institutions. Anarchism attracts him intellectually. He delights in being iconoclastic and provocative: "The religion of duty has replaced the religion of idols. . . .Science [has replaced] metaphysics" (I, 168). The social revolution, the law of progress, the advance of humanity, these are the new watchwords. He repudiates all false values, be they literary or political, and proclaims his independence: "I do not hesitate to go against the general run of fools. I prefer the discreet approbation of a few cultured persons to the routine applause of the *sensible elements*" (I, 63). During this first period the influence upon him of European, especially French, writers is evident. The reader who is familiar with the books written by Azorín during the first quarter of the twentieth century may find this proto-Azorín almost unrecognizable. And yet, beneath all the sound and fury there are intimations of his future: the theme of Spain—its landscape and history—is already present, and from Azorín's comments on other writers much can be deduced about his own aesthetic credo. He stresses the importance of clarity and naturalness of style, attention to detail, and careful observation, praises the use of short chapters of two or three pages which the reader can easily follow, and speaks of the charm of digressions.

I   The Valencian Years

Azorín's first published work was *La crítica literaria en España* (Literary Criticism in Spain, 1893). It is a "state of the art" report on Spanish literary criticism, which he divides into two branches. The first of these is historical, the patient investigation of past works and periods. In passing, he criticizes the fragmentation of historical studies and advocates a new type of history which would embrace all aspects of life (politics, letters, science, customs, commerce, etc.) and give a true picture of Spanish civilization. In later years he will often take this comprehensive approach in his reconstructions of the past. The second type of criticism, consisting of "impressions of the moment" written in response to the reading of a new book, will be cultivated by Azorín throughout his career.

Despite stylistic weaknesses, *Literary Criticism* is valuable for several reasons. Azorín's review of what has been done and what remains to be done in the way of historical criticism reveals him to be, at age nineteen, exceptionally well read. And, from the perspective of 1893, his conclusion that Spanish criticism in general suffers from a lack of penetration and an excess of rhetoric is justified. Few critics emerge unscathed from his review of their work, and he tosses more brickbats than bouquets. He describes the respected critic Clarín as neither a genius nor a mediocrity, adding that while "no one will deny his vast and sound erudition, which he at times abuses" (I, 23), he lacks impartiality and consistency.[1]

Azorín's second pamphlet, a sketch of the eighteenth-century dramatist Moratín, is included in the 1894 book *Buscapiés* (Squibs), along with sixteen new pieces. In a truculent prologue Ahrimán declares that sincerity is a rarity in Spain and that those brave souls who dare to openly voice their criticism are subjected to numerous annoyances. Satirical writers are anathema to the "respectable" elements of society and run the danger of being challenged to duels by those they have offended, or of being denounced by the public prosecutor. *Squibs* is a heterogeneous collection of satires and criticisms. The novelist and critic Emilia Pardo Bazán is savaged in a mock necrology, and in "Los ideales de antaño" (The Ideals of Yesteryear) the exaggerated scruples of eighteenth-century moralists are ridiculed. Present-day Spain is characterized as possibly the most backward country in Europe. Freedom of the press and of worship do not exist; if they did, the Monarchy would topple. The Royal Spanish Academy is filled with "esteemed mummies" (I, 90); the Church is a vendor of spiritual beverages. Several of the sketches show the influence of writers admired by Azorín. "Hastío" (Disgust) is reminiscent of Larra's "El día de difuntos de 1836" (All Souls' Day, 1836). Here a melancholy Ahrimán tries to relieve his spleen by seeking refuge in his books, only to discover that two of his country's most famous playwrights bore him. He turns to Shakespeare in search of the profundity, passion, and psychological insight lacking in Spanish dramatists, but the Spanish translation is so awkward that he bursts into laughter.

During the Valencian years Azorín also wrote polemic works which were more politically oriented. *Anarquistas literarios* (Literary Anarchists, 1895) is dedicated to the French sociologist Augustin Hamon. As defined by Azorín, anarchists are those men of independent spirit who love liberty, justice, and their fellow men and have a highly developed moral sensibility. This very broad definition permits the inclusion of Socrates, Plato, the Spanish monarch Charles III, and Pope Gregory I within the ranks of the anarchists. In the field of literature, those who "have the courage to write what and how they feel, without heeding ridiculous traditions or fearing the avenging thunderbolts of false gods" (I, 156) also merit the name of anarchists. They protest all that is irrational and all assaults on individual freedom. In the second part of *Literary Anarchists* Azorín enumerates the obstacles which stand in the way of the triumph of the social revolution in Spain: the apathy of the people, the strength of the Church and the Army, the decay of agriculture and industry, the corruption of politics, the absence of widespread public education, and the frivolity and partisanship of the press. He exhorts his countrymen to dedicate themselves to education, scientific studies, and hard work. In the pamphlet *Notas sociales* (Social Notes, 1895) a similar exhortation is addressed to young Spanish writers. Azorín urges them to cooperate in the task of regenerating their society and to view literature as a weapon to be wielded in defense of noble ideals. In both these works he espouses anarchist ideology.[2]

The two essays contained in *Literatura* (Literature, 1896) consist of brief comments on contemporary Spanish authors. Of particular interest are observations on what will be one of Azorín's major concerns: the problem of how the artist can best portray reality. Should he attempt to imitate everything and, if not, what norm should be follow in deciding what is to be excluded? He insists that the writer, like the painter, must know how to "see." In connection with this remark he praises Flaubert: "His descriptions are always truthful; his details, precise and essential. As an observer of great power, he always finds the detail necessary for the evocation of a thing or a character" (I, 219). In a later book Azorín will elaborate on the decisive importance of the small, suggestive detail which has the power to evoke an entire state of consciousness.

Further evidence of Azorín's concerns during these years is furnished by the translations he published in 1896 and 1897: lectures by Hamon ("On the Fatherland") and by the Russian social philosopher Peter Kropotkin ("Prisons"), and the play *The Intruder* by the Belgian Maurice Maeterlinck. The first two translations are a logical outgrowth of Azorín's interest in anarchism. With regard to the third, he published an article praising *The Intruder* as an example of "static" theater, the type of theater he would cultivate some thirty years later. In the play "nothing 'happens'; there are no shouts or imprecations; there are no deaths, betrayals, adulteries; but there is something which takes possession of the spirit and makes the soul tremble with the vibration of the unknown and of the tragic. Things speak: the leaves of the trees in the garden, the door which refuses to close, the moonbeam which pierces the stained-glass windows, the lamp which slowly goes out, the cry of the weeping child."[3]

II   *Early Years in Madrid*

Upon arriving in Madrid in 1896 Azorín began contributing to *El País*. Many of the newspaper's subscribers were shocked by his aggressively anticlerical, anarchistic views, attacks on marriage, and defense of divorce and free love, and their complaints led to his being dropped from the staff of the paper in February 1897. The next few months were difficult ones. It is not clear to what extent his family was still aiding him financially, but Azorín claimed that he subsisted for several weeks on twenty cents worth of bread a day. Later that same year he published *Charivari*, explaining that this title was chosen because the work is "passionate, discordant, chaotic" (I, 243). It takes the form of a supposed diary with entries dating from November 25, 1896, through April 2, 1897, and incorporates some of Azorín's *El País* articles. Much of the work is a self-serving diatribe in which he takes revenge on the world of journalism. He condescendingly describes the editorial staff of *El País* as lazy, incompetent, given to clichés—and he mentions the praise his own articles have received. He had prefaced one of the essays in *Literature* with a quotation from Larra to the effect that although he neither seeks nor avoids polemics, he will always carefully avoid personal matters and intrusions into the private lives of others, out of a sense of decorum and respect for them. Decorum and respect, however, are missing in a number of the entries in *Charivari*. Particularly virulent is the attack on the popular playwright Joaquín Dicenta. Azorín stoops to allusions to Dicenta's drinking habits, the low company he keeps, and his mistress. The publication of *Charivari* quite understandably caused a furor, and according to one anecdote Azorín narrowly escaped a thrashing at the hands of Dicenta. Fearing that those whom he had verbally abused might respond with physical abuse, Azorín disappeared from Madrid until the uproar had died down.

Also published in 1897 was a collection of short stories entitled *Bohemia*. The first, "Fragmentos de un diario" (Fragments from a Diary), is similar in tone and form to *Charivari* and is the most directly autobiographical. A series of entries for the month of March portrays the suffering occasioned by Azorín's financial difficulties. Apparently still smarting over his dismissal from *El País*, he again mentions the praise his newspaper pieces have received both from eminent men of letters and anonymous readers.

Several of the stories in *Bohemia* reflect a certain bitterness and disillusionment with the literary world. The petty rivalries, backbiting, and the fear felt by established writers who regard the new generation as a threat are evident in "El maestro" (The Master) and "El amigo" (The Friend). In both, a modest, ingenuous young writer of talent is betrayed by an older writer who professes to be sincerely interested in helping him. The protagonist of "Una vida" (A Life) is a nonconformist who is bitterly reproached by his bourgeois family for his harebrained ideas, i.e., his rebellion against convention. His almost total physical paralysis is symptomatic of his powerlessness to change society and impose on it his humanitarian ideals. At the end of the story he commits suicide while his family serenely watches. The protagonist is termed *el enfermo* (the sick man), but it is clear that his "loving" family and society are the real *enfermos*. The most macabre of the tales is "Una mujer" (A Woman), whose main character calmly allows the lover of whom she is tiring to be buried alive. These four stories are mini-dramas, complete with stage directions and division into scenes. Azorín apparently felt that in each case the anecdote would have greater impact and immediacy if expressed in dialogue form and without authorial comment or emotional outpourings. In these tales he comes closest to achieving his goal of crystalline clarity and naturalness.

Azorín's interest in the Castilian landscape and the relationship between the land and those who inhabit it surfaces in *Bohemia*, as does his antiurbanism. The main character of "Paisajes" (Landscapes) is a young man who dreams of writing a book into which he will pour his love of nature and depict the states of mind and sensations it inspires. But he falls victim to the corrupting atmosphere of a large city and wastes his time and energy leading a Bohemian life.

Soledades (Solitudes, 1898) is a miscellaneous collection of stories, aphorisms, and observations on a variety of subjects. Criticism of the selfishness and hypocrisy of the literary world continues, and Azorín bemoans the misfortune of those who have to struggle to win fame in a country where established writers refuse to concede the merit of their young rivals. In a sketch which closely resembles Larra's "Yo quiero ser cómico" (I Want to Be an Actor), a young man seeks advice as to what career to follow. After discovering that the youth has no sense of shame or dignity and knows absolutely nothing about literature or art, his interlocutor recommends that he become a journalist. In another sketch, the wealthy writer Fernando refuses to even read a letter sent him by a fellow writer who is dying of tuberculosis, a man Fernando claims to love like a brother.

The satiric pamphlet *Pecuchet, demagogo* (Pecuchet, Demagogue, 1898) is one of the more interesting early works because of what it shows about its author. He portrays Pecuchet as a man who prides himself on being *the* revolutionary, the model of honesty and consistency who has dedicated his life to defending his ideas, and those ideas are summed up in his implacable hatred of the Jesuits. In reality, Pecuchet is an anticlerical reactionary who in the name of Progress displays all the intolerance of a Torquemada and who uses his newspaper *El Escándalo* to excoriate the Church. A former disciple accuses the demagogue of not realizing that consistency means being irrevocably committed to always holding the same opinion regardless of the changes which have taken place in the world, and that it is the greatest enemy of independence. In light of Azorín's own frequent about-faces this criticism of consistency and implied defense of apostasy is revealing. *Pecuchet, Demagogue* is itself an example of one of Azorín's curious reversals. It is generally accepted that the main target of this attack on a pseudorevolutionary is José Nakens, publisher of the newspaper *El Motín*. Only a few months previously Azorín had held up Nakens as an example to Spanish youth, praising him as a man of great and generous heart and lauding the sincerity of his revolutionary convictions.

From the spring of 1898 until the autumn of 1899 Azorín temporarily abandons his journalistic career and at his family's urging resumes his law studies, albeit halfheartedly. Although he never obtained a degree, the respite from journalism was productive in other ways. He began working on *Diary of a Sick Man* and in 1899 published *La evolución de la crítica* (The Evolution of Criticism) and *La sociología criminal* (Criminal Sociology). This last work is a treatise on the doctrines of various criminologists and penologists. Azorín traces the gradual recognition of the importance of socioeconomic factors as the cause of crime and denies that society has the right to punish criminal behavior. *The Evolution of Criticism* is an attempt to disseminate in Spain critical theories already well known in other nations. The subject of the generally low level of Spanish culture leads into an excursus on the country's history. Azorín charges that the Catholic Sovereigns Ferdinand and Isabella achieved national unity by stifling all regional liberties and giving free rein to the Inquisition. As a result Spain becomes "a beautiful country of theologians, soldiers, and whores" (I, 406). The rulers of the House of Austria pursue a quixotic policy both in the New World and in the Old, where they attempt to "right the wrongs" of the Reformation. "Afterwards, defeated, impoverished, and with Spain depopulated by wars, hunger, and the expulsion of the Jews, ruin is rapid and total" (I, 407). And the Bourbons carry the process of decadence one step further. Both in literature and in science men of talent become the exception and universities are the seat of ignorance and pedantry. The preceding obviously conflicts with the "official" interpretation of Spanish history but is representative of the early views propounded by the Generation of 1898.

III   *A Turning Point*

1900 and 1901 mark the final stage of Azorín's literary apprenticeship. *El alma castellana (1600-1800)* (The Castilian Soul) is
devoted to what will be one of the main features of subsequent
books, the reconstruction of the past, and it exemplifies the all-
embracing type of history which Azorín had called for in *Literary
Criticism in Spain*.[4] He sets the scene for his recreation of life in
the seventeenth century by describing the state of the economy:
costly wars have led to ever-increasing taxes and a devaluation of
the currency; agriculture has been neglected; industry has declined; and commerce is scorned as beneath the dignity of men of
honor. This serves as the background for chapters which deal with
domestic life, love, fashion, picaresque life, the Inquisition, the
theater, convents, mysticism, men of letters, and Castilian prose.

Azorín figuratively transports his readers into the past, enabling
them temporarily to inhabit another age, and he frequently refers
to and quotes from works of the period he is evoking. He praises as
of inestimable historical value the *Curioso tratado de la natura-
leza y calidad del chocolate* (Curious Treatise on the Nature and
Quality of Chocolate), 1631, and passes on its author's instructions
as to how to prepare this exotic new beverage. Details about femi-
nine makeup, hair styles, and dress or about the debate on the pros
and cons of the use of tobacco, seen by some as the consolation of
mankind and by others as an invention of Satan which literally
scorches one's insides, help capture the flavor of the past.

The Castilian Soul contains a chilling description of the spectacle of an auto-da-fé during the reign of Charles II, but also a
warm tribute to a different type of religiosity: "The most energetic, greatest, most Spanish souls of past centuries are found in
monasteries. . . .Spanish mysticism is not inactive, silent, and
self-absorbed in the great solitary cloisters; it is a combative, rest-
less, roving, proselytizing religion" (I, 636-37). Comments on literature are also included. It is seen as an expression of the adven-
turous spirit of the times. The emphasis upon action explains the
flourishing of the theater and even of Baroque poetry, for according to Azorín the latter's endless images and conceits reflect the
desire to display dexterity and overcome obstacles. The section on
life in the 1700s is briefer. Azorín finds much that meets with his
approval: the new thirst for knowledge, renewed contact with
other countries and circulation of foreign works, the growing pro-

fessionalism of the press. There is also much that is not to his liking: increasing governmental regulation of life, licentious customs, and the ludicrously rigid rules of conduct formulated by moralists.

An offshoot of the research for *The Castilian Soul* is the tragicomedy *La fuerza del amor* (The Power of Love, 1901). Set in 1636, the action recalls that of many Baroque dramas. The noble but poor Don Fernando de Tavera has fallen in love with Doña Aurelia, who has agreed to marry the wealthy Don Félix de Guevara and thus save her father from financial ruin. Fernando gains entry to Aurelia's home by feigning madness, declaring that he is the famous knight-errant Amadís de Gaula. Tolerated as a figure of fun, he is able to declare his love for Aurelia and insult his rival Don Félix with impunity. At the play's conclusion the hero fights Félix for the lady and emerges triumphant. Azorín carefully documents his recreation of the early seventeenth century and following each of the first three acts lists his sources, which include *Don Quixote*, *Amadis of Gaul*, the *Celestina*, jokebooks, and accounts of events of the 1630s. Pastiches of passages from various picaresque novels and of Don Quixote's discourse on arms and letters are incorporated in the script. In the play Azorín repeats many of the curious details about seventeenth-century customs which had appeared in *The Castilian Soul* and again alludes to the lamentable economic condition of the nation.

Many of the characters are not original creations but literary types: the braggart soldier, the pedantic doctor, the wise "madman," the "saintly" eremite who turns out to be a cardsharp, the gullible student who is duped into providing a free meal for the rogues at an inn, and a Celestinesque go-between. The opening scenes at the inn and some of Fernando's sallies are amusing, but the play was never staged since the size of the cast and the lavish sets and costumes made that impractical. *The Power of Love* is well summed up by Baroja's unenthusiastic but polite comment: "nice, well-documented, discreet" (I, 738). Baroja devotes most of his prologue to the play to a defense and portrait of Azorín. He explains that although his friend has been accused of being tortuous and inconsistent, he is not really so. Instead of adhering to a preconceived plan of life, Azorín has modified that plan as his ideas and feelings have changed. He has been consistent with himself if not with others. Baroja also calls attention to the contrast between the outer and inner man. "He is impressionable to the point of exaggeration, and his eyes are inexpressive; he is nervous and yet appears impassive; his words are fiery, and his face is cold and his gestures automatic" (I, 738).

As in *Charivari* and the first story of *Bohemia*, the diary form is used in what is the key composition of the 1893-1901 period, the novelette *Diario de un enfermo* (Diary of a Sick Man, 1901). Its nameless protagonist repeatedly glimpses and finally meets a woman who is identified only as *ella*. Tall, blond, pale, always dressed in black, her eyes seem fixed upon infinity and there is an ineffable sadness in her gaze. The protagonist marries this ideal being, only to have her die less than two months later. In the original version the disconsolate husband commits suicide, but at Azorín's request this ending was omitted from the *Complete Works*.[5] With the exception of this sentimental fiction, the novelette is largely autobiographical in the sense that the personal, aesthetic, and philosophical questions over which the protagonist mulls are ones which preoccupy his creator. In *Diary* are found what will be the basic concerns of Azorín's subsequent fiction: time, the conflict between action and contemplation, the relationship between art and reality, and the creative process.[6] Here appear ideas on the novel which will be more fully articulated in *Will*.

Under the guise of publisher of his "friend's" diary, Azorín urges in a prefatory note that these pages be read religiously, for in them "throbs the spirit of an anguished artist" (I, 691). The sensitive, introspective protagonist pours out his metaphysical anguish and Romantic pessimism, resorting to frequent exclamations, rhetorical questions, and the use of italics for emphasis. Like his creator, he is tormented by the question of what type of existence to pursue, the reflective or the active. Would it not be better to participate directly in life rather than to experience it at one remove in books? Watching a couple dancing, clasped in each other's arms, he wonders if he is not an imbecile to spend his time reading philosophy. "Where is life: in books or in the street? . . . Let us live, let us live. The great artists *created* because they *lived*" (I, 695). And a week later he writes: "I have spent the morning on my historical research. . . .Is not this stupid, incredibly stupid, inhuman, incredibly inhuman? . . .No more books; no more dusty printed pages, catalogues of dead sensations, indices of others' lives!" (I, 695-96). And yet if he were to embrace life would not his art suffer? Would he not have to forego the pleasure afforded by the leisurely savoring of sensations? His perception of the passage of time accentuates his melancholy and leads him to reflect that the pursuit of fame is pointless, for "nothing is eternal; everything changes, everything passes away, everything perishes" (I, 694).

His inner turmoil continues as he questions the objective reality of the surrounding world and of existence itself. "Do we perhaps exist? Is not *that which is objective* a hallucination of our senses? . . .Yes; perhaps reality is an illusion, and we ourselves are illusions which float for a moment and disappear into Nothingness, also a chimera" (I, 705). Behind the diarist's musings lie Azorín's sense of dissatisfaction with his life to date and his skepticism as to whether his militant radicalism has accomplished anything. Significant as an indication of the future orientation of his writing are the qualities which the protagonist admires in the mystic Santa Teresa de Jesús: "the profoundly artistic detachment from earthly things, the yearning for the infinite, the serene, unswerving flight toward the Ideal" (I, 720).

The diarist's reflections on the shortcomings of literature lead him to the formulation of a new aesthetic. As earlier artists failed to understand nature, present-day writers err in concerning themselves with the extraordinary and abnormal. They fail to comprehend the aesthetic of repose, the deep and moving tragedy of a moment of silence—and *Diary* is filled with such moments—or how much can be conveyed by a nuance or half-gesture. The ability to express sensations has not kept pace with the ability to perceive them; hence the frustration of the artist, which could be compared to that of a watchmaker who has at his disposal only a hammer and saw instead of the precise implements which he needs. Again and again Azorín will return to this topic of the inadequacies of language, the writer's tool.

During the months covered by the diary, November 1898 to April 1900, the protagonist makes several excursions from Madrid. The most important is the one to Toledo. It enables Azorín to pay homage to a city which greatly impressed the writers of the Generation of 1898 and to one of their favorite artists, El Greco. And while in Toledo the protagonist converses with an old friend who has abandoned his literary career for politics and in the process has lost his former delicate sensibility and idealism. The friend's figurative death, the result of choosing action over contemplation, foreshadows the protagonist's end.[7]

In his analysis of *Diary*, Leon Livingstone notes that it has ele-

ments of a prenovel (the material remains inchoate), of an anti-
novel (the incompleteness is deliberate), and of a novel-within-a-
novel.[8] It is an example of interior duplication. The author-
protagonist of the diary is a literary projection of the real author.
The former is engaged in the process of writing the same type of
novel as the latter has written. The protagonist's description of his
work as "chapters of an inchoate novel, fragments of an initiated
intimate history" (I, 693) can also be applied to Azorín's *Diary of a
Sick Man*. In it Azorín cultivates the aesthetic of repose recommended by his character, an aesthetic which "decrees that the
function of art is the translation of sensibility rather than the
narration of action-situation."[9] In accord with this new aesthetic
Azorín develops the technique of the arrested moment, extracting
a moment from the stream of time so that it can be contemplated
in tranquility.

CHAPTER 3

Success and Maturity: I. Novels

THE reader who had been brought up on the realistic-naturalistic fiction of the latter part of the nineteenth century was accustomed to a well-developed plot and to a fairly complete narration of the life of the protagonist. The latter's physical appearance, dress, mannerisms, family background, and his external world were usually described in detail. The publication in 1902 of Baroja's *The Way to Perfection*, Unamuno's *Amor y pedagogía* (Love and Pedagogy), Valle-Inclán's *Sonata de otoño* (Autumn Sonata), and Azorín's *Will* signaled a rejection of the old novelistic canons. These new novels relegated plot to a position of secondary importance and were more concerned with the inner drama of the characters than with their outer appearance. Objectivity and impersonality were no longer sacrosanct. On the contrary, the author's personality, his ideas, and his subjective response to the world around him were now important elements of the novel. The former more or less clear-cut distinctions among novel, essay, and poetry became blurred as the novelist shared his sensibility with the reader and incorporated into his work disquisitions on philosophy, religion, history, political and social theories, or aesthetics.

In *Will* Azorín affirms that the novel as practiced by the preceding generation falls far short of perfection. Its descriptions, dialogue, and structure are deficient. In his opinion, the measure of the true artist is his feeling for nature, his ability to interpret the "emotion of the landscape." He must capture its emotional resonance rather than just reproduce it, and he must find the suggestive detail. Even more false than the descriptive passages of the traditional novel are its dialogues, for they are too literary. In real life people speak incoherently, incorrectly, with frequent pauses and in short sentences. And the very plot and structure of the traditional novel is a falsification of reality. "Above all, there should not be a plot...; life does not have a plot; it is diverse, multiform, undulating, contradictory..., everything except symmetrical, geometrical, rigid, as it appears in novels" (I, 864). It is ridiculous to attempt to recount everything a character does from morning to night, for what is meaningful may be extracted and condensed into a few sensations which will represent the essence of his life. "*All* life cannot be contained in one volume, and if we give ten, twenty, forty sensations, that is enough" (I, 864). In Azorín's hands the novel becomes primarily lyrical and descriptive, and there is no systematic narration of incident and consequence.

I   La voluntad *(Will)*

Antonio Azorín, the protagonist of *La voluntad* (Will), is seen as a symbol of the youth of his time.[1] He is a man of contradictions, torn asunder by the conflict between the two different beings who coexist within him. One, the man of will, has been almost destroyed by the inhibiting influence of his education in a religious school, the environment of Yecla, and the teachings of his mentor Yuste. His other self, the man of reflection and self-analysis, is dominant. The novel portrays the steady disintegration of Antonio's will and at the same time documents the intellectual and spiritual crisis of the end of the nineteenth century. Azorín has projected his own state of mind and many of his personal concerns into the figure of Antonio, and a number of the novel's episodes are based upon Azorín's own experiences (the 1900 trip to Toledo, the 1901 pilgrimage to Larra's tomb, the 1902 banquet honoring Baroja), but these elements have been elaborated artistically. There are numerous discrepancies between the real life of the author and that of his literary projection. *Will* has been aptly described as the novel of what might have happened to Azorín.[2]

In *Valencia* he recalled that his first novels were characterized as incoherent by critics who failed to see beneath the surface (VI, 46). Actually, *Will* is a carefully thought out and coherent work. In the prologue Azorín introduces the concept of eternal recurrence—which is subsequently elaborated on by Yuste and Antonio—and a key to the character of Antonio. The prologue is an account of the building of a church in Yecla. Despite the fervor of the people, work on the project was sporadic, and periods of energetic activity alternated with others of inaction. The pace of the construction is paralleled by that of the narrative. The dynamism of the first paragraphs of the prologue with their many verbs and short, juxtaposed phrases gives way to a slower rhythm of longer clauses.[3] The oscillating, ever slower movement of the construction of the church is analogous to the pattern of Antonio's life, a series of fits and starts. In the epilogue of the novel the unfinished cathedral is explicitly linked to the unfinished man Antonio, "un hombre *sin acabar*" (I, 991). In the concluding paragraph of the prologue the narrator stresses that the present is a repetition of the past. Twenty-five centuries earlier the same religious fervor led to the construction of a pagan temple which dominated the city of Elo as the new church dominates Yecla. The same quarry provided stone for both edifices. In both, similar rites were performed and the faithful sought consolation for the sorrows of mankind. In the course of history, externals change, but the underlying essence of human experience remains the same. And in the course of the novel, the concept of cyclical time is illustrated by the repetition of motifs, events, and situations.[4]

In Part I of the novel the narrator portrays the physical and intellectual environment which has molded the character of the protagonist. Antonio remains a somewhat shadowy figure. In many of the chapters his role is limited to that of interjecting an occasional comment or question into the discourses of the skeptic Yuste. Those discourses range over a variety of topics. Yuste rails against private property as the root of all evil and maintains that the existing social order must be completely changed, discusses the problem of the emigration of peasants to the city and the disappearance of small agricultural holdings, and sums up the late nineteenth century as an era of venal politicians, bombastic writers, and general vulgarity. He also reflects on how fleeting literary glory is. The words of Yuste in conjunction with the oppressive, death-ridden atmosphere of Yecla incline Antonio toward an increasingly pessimistic view of the world.

The characters of the novel are frequently grouped in similar or contrasting pairs. There are two quixotic inventors, two representatives of the *pueblo*, two teachers and two disciples, Yuste's influence on Antonio being paralleled by that of the cleric Puche on his niece Justina. The weak-willed Justina, to whom Antonio is attracted, is set against the domineering Iluminada, who is bent on marrying Antonio. In Part II Antonio is paired with another young writer, Olaiz, who represents the author's friend Baroja. This technique is also applied to the arrangement of chapters. Chapters 2 and 3, for example, are structurally parallel. Each begins with a long description of a house. On the facade of Puche's residence a large cross stands out, and religious prints adorn the walls of the living room. Similarly, Yuste's study is filled with books, among which stand out three volumes by Schopenhauer. In these settings Justina and Antonio listen attentively to the words of their respective mentors. Puche's Christian stoicism contrasts with Yuste's skepticism, but the two differing ideological positions lead to the same annihilation of the will.[5] Under the influence of her uncle, Justina turns her back on the world and enters a convent, where she dies, and at the end of the novel Antonio is married to Iluminada and figuratively dead. This fate is foreshadowed in Part I by Antonio's reflection that he would never have the energy to oppose Iluminada's wishes and, after all, why should he? By taking him in tow she would be doing him the immense favor of living half of his life for him.

Following the death of Yuste and Justina, Antonio abandons Yecla for Madrid. The spectacle of the frivolity which dominates all spheres of life in the capital reinforces his instinctive pessimism. The theme of "vanity of vanities, all is vanity" runs throughout Part II. Yuste's earlier observations on the venality of politicians and the empty phrases of journalists are echoed by Antonio's reflections that there is nothing more abject than a politician and that journalists are no better. An afternoon spent in the National Library leafing through old newspapers and photographs of the 1860-1870 decade brings home Yuste's point about the transience of fame.

As in Part I teacher and disciple had strolled through Yecla and the surrounding countryside, in Part II Antonio strolls through Madrid and visits nearby cities. In Toledo he meditates on the relationship between the Spanish landscape and the Spanish character. The harshness of the land and its violent contrasts have shaped the character of its inhabitants, making them austere and inflexible. The sadness of the land and of the people informs Spanish art. Toledo, "somber, deserted, tragic" (I, 920), fascinates Antonio, but he finds Madrid totally repellent. Its residents are caught up in a frenzied *danse macabre*. Life in the capital is a "nightmare of Lust, Pain and Death" (I, 917). In Part II Antonio's intellectual and ethical disorientation increases, and in the last chapter of this section he is described as representative of "an entire generation without will, without energy, indecisive, irresolute" (I, 959).

In Part II of *Will* Antonio moves into the foreground, but, as in Part I, he is seen through the eyes of the narrator, who maintains a degree of distance from his characters. In Part III the reader is given an inside view of Antonio. So that "the complex psychology of this perplexed spirit" (I, 961) may be seen more clearly, the narrator steps aside and presents the reader with fragments jotted down by Antonio in his spare time. This change to a first-person point of view gives greater immediacy to the character's predicament. Antonio here defines himself as a man in rebellion against himself. "I am a man of my time! Intelligence has developed at the expense of will" (I, 968); "aboulia paralyzes my will" (I, 974). He still has an occasional outburst of anger, but more and more he falls into a state of indifference. Even books have lost their appeal. The humane thing, he reflects, would be to put an end to human suffering by putting an end to the species. Eventually he decides to return to Yecla, envisioning his life there as an empty round of trivial conversations at the casino or club and arguments about the merits of local politicians and third-rate writers.

The epilogue of the novel consists of three letters written by J. Martínez Ruiz to Pío Baroja regarding their former companion Antonio. It thus introduces into the fictional world of the character the real world of Martínez Ruiz and Baroja, "transforming into reality what up to that moment was received by the reader as imaginary."[6] The letters reveal the extent to which Antonio has been eclipsed by his wife. He is no longer "Don Antonio Azorín" but simply "Antoñico, the man who is married to Doña Iluminada" (I, 983). The second and third letters emphasize the representative value of both Yecla and Antonio. The city's recent history is seen as emblematic of what has happened in much of Spain. The upper-class families have squandered their money and neglected their holdings. The sons of the middle-class families have turned from agriculture to the pursuit of bureaucratic careers, and the cultivation of the land has been left to the most inept. The mentality of the visionary who conceives projects but never carries them through to conclusion prevails in Yecla. The city is disintegrating. It is not surprising that Antonio, born and educated in this environment, should suffer from passivity and lack of will. "His case, more or less, is that of all Spanish youth" (I, 990). Will Antonio continue to vegetate in Yecla? Martínez Ruiz suggests that perhaps not. "An interesting volume could be written about his past life, and I hope that perhaps another titled *The Second Life of Antonio Azorín* can be written" (I, 995).

Forty years later Azorín declared that he had not conceived *Will* as a thesis novel but as a reaction against an environment.[7] It is essentially a protest novel by an angry young man who denounces the political, social, and moral situation of Spain. The ideological element predominates. The story line is tenuous. Potential sources of dramatic interest, such as the relationship between Justina and Antonio, are presented obliquely. Dialogues are replaced by monologues punctuated by moments of silence. Azorín deliberately avoids traditional narrative procedures. The fragments and sensations which make up the novel are not, however, without pattern. Symmetrical grouping, structural parallelism, and recapitulation provide coherence. Changes in point of view serve to present the reader with complementary images of the protagonist. The narrator's external, often belittling vision is replaced by the internal, subjective vision of the protagonist, which in turn yields to the sympathetic vision of the extraliterary Martínez Ruiz. Prologue and epilogue point up the parallel between the unfinished cathedral and the unfinished man, both "products" of Yecla. Spatially, the novel moves in a circle, and Antonio's return to Yecla and Iluminada exemplifies the cyclic pattern of existence.

Azorín carefully documented much of the descriptive material presented in *Will*. Months of research in the library of the Instituto de San Isidro provided information which was utilized in the portrayal of Justina's life in a convent. Before writing the novel's opening description of dawn in Yecla, Azorín got up before daybreak and from the vantage point of a hill overlooking the city jotted down all the details he needed. Visual and auditory sensations predominate in the passage. The crowing of cocks, barking of dogs, braying of donkeys, and ringing of bells signal the awakening of the city. As the sky brightens, objects slowly emerge out of the darkness, and colors change. Azorín shared the Impressionists' interest in direct observation of nature and the study of light and its refractions, and in his description he employs words borrowed from the vocabulary of painting: *esfumar* (to stump or tone down), *mancha* (spot or patch [of color]), and *pincelada* (brushstroke).[8]

II   Antonio Azorín

The closing paragraph of *Will* held out the hope of a "second life" for Antonio. The 1903 novel *Antonio Azorín* is not the chronological continuation of the first volume but an alternative version and, like the first, is not to be read as the literal autobiography of the author. Parts I and II are set in Monóvar and Petrel, Part III in Madrid— where Antonio seeks fame as a writer—and in Castilian towns where he reflects on the decadence of Spain. With the exception of the protagonist, the cast of characters is new, and the Antonio of this second novel is unmarried. In the dedication, J.M.R. presents himself as the chronicler of the life of his friend and apologizes for the insubstantiality of the book. He explains by way of justification that Antonio is an ordinary man to whom nothing extraordinary, such as an adulterous love or a duel, ever happens. Neither dramatic action nor profound thoughts can be expected from such an individual. Through the use of irony the chronicler dissociates himself from his subject. The impression of separation between the two is enhanced in Parts I and II of the novel, where the chronicler gently makes fun of Antonio and presents him indirectly in terms of the environments in which he moves.

The initial chapters of the novel describe in miniaturistic detail the valley of Elda and the country house of Antonio. The setting is seen as if through the eye of a movie camera which slowly moves over the valley before focusing on the house and on the study in particular, where each photograph and piece of furniture is scrutinized. At last the camera moves on to the bedroom. Again there is a scrutiny of the furniture, including an armchair in which Antonio is seated unpacking a suitcase. This detailed presentation of the setting serves a definite purpose. Since, according to Azorín, man is shaped by his environment, that environment must be carefully portrayed. Furthermore, since Antonio's house is an extension of his personality, the description of the house serves as an indirect description of its inhabitant. Later the scene shifts to Antonio's residence in Monóvar and the room where he meditates and suffers his "dreadful spiritual torments" (I, 1028). Again the camera moves through the house, slowly approaches Antonio, lingers for a moment, and moves on. The chronicler gives his subject a quick sidelong glance and then veers off into a generalization about the tedious and repetitive nature of provincial life.

This topic is developed in a series of vignettes of nameless characters: an old woman who is obsessed with death, an old man who has organized an amateur theatrical group, elderly peasants who exchange a few laconic remarks about the weather, the habitués of the local casino, and a solemn old man who has written the libretto for several musical comedies. The chronicler observes that in the towns of Spain life is monotonous and yet is clung to more tenaciously than in the cities. The presentation of these anonymous figures further fills out the picture of the milieu which has influenced Antonio. Detailed descriptions of exteriors and interiors have shown how that environment looks, and sketches of life in the provinces have demonstrated how that environment affects the people who move within it. A long letter from Antonio's uncle, Pascual Verdú, provides the finishing touches of the picture and offers a glimpse of the provincial literary and political scene.[9]

In Part I Antonio is little more than an episodic figure. In Part II he and the individuals with whom he comes in contact receive greater attention. Most influential are his new mentors Verdú and Sarrió. The "education" they provide differs from that furnished by Yuste in *Will*, and their outlook is more positive. Just as Yuste's somber dwelling was in tune with its inhabitant's gloomy views, Verdú's house is bright and airy. He is a man of both intelligence and faith, as intimated by the description of his study where there are numerous books and an image of the Virgin. The fact that a world of ideas separates Antonio from Verdú is unimportant. What matters is Verdú's openness, tolerance, and generosity. In *Antonio Azorín* a new importance is attributed to affective values, goodness, and compassion. Intellectual endowments are no longer all important. This is demonstrated by Antonio's friendship with Sarrió. Short, fat, with dancing eyes and red cheeks, Sarrió is an epicurean, more interested in good food and fine wine than in intellectual matters. His reading appears to be limited to cookbooks. It is he who reveals to Antonio the simple pleasures of daily life. Antonio shares neither Verdú's religious faith nor Sarrió's vitality and intense enjoyment of life, but he respects his friends' ideas. He is also drawn to Sarrió's vivacious daughter Pepita, who is quite unlike the colorless Justina or the overbearing Iluminada of *Will*. The beneficial influences of Verdú, Sarrió, and Pepita help explain the change visible in this second Antonio. He is less radical and irritable, more tolerant.

This more affirmative attitude toward life can be seen in a comparison of certain subjects which are discussed in both the 1902 and 1903 novels: politicians, the casino, the clergy, and the conflicts between generations. In *Will* politicians were described as the most contemptible and repugnant of creatures. In *Antonio Azorín* the politicians themselves are no less stupid, but they are regarded with ironic amusement rather than rage. The casino, an important part of life in the towns of Spain, is viewed in the 1902 novel as a symbol of the intellectual sterility and narrowness of the provinces, but in *Antonio Azorín* it is judged less harshly. The elderly, respectable gentlemen of Monóvar gather in the casino to discuss what is going on in a "discreet and peaceful conversation" (I, 1046) or to talk about the good old days. It is the nostalgia of the old for the past rather than the triviality of the conversations that is stressed.

In the two novels there are a number of clergymen. In *Will* most of them are somber and ascetic; the clergy of *Antonio Azorín* do not deny the possibility of earthly happiness and are more sympathetically portrayed.[10] The chronicler comments in regard to one cleric that he, "like many others, merits our respect and even our admiration" (I, 1045). Particularly important is the bishop of Orihuela. He is a well-read, unpretentious, likable man who loves all that God has created. He is perturbed by modern philosophers (Nietzsche, Schopenhauer, Stirner) who are leading the young astray as books of chivalry did Don Quixote. Everything in life, he maintains, has its reason for being, but the young lack that humble vision of things, that understanding of reality which Alonso Quijano attained on his deathbed.

Both Yuste and Verdú comment on literary fame. Yuste sadly observes how ephemeral it is and how rapidly tastes change. Verdú regards these changes in a more positive light. Human sensibility, he declares, becomes more refined as time passes and therefore man's concept of what is beautiful alters. Younger writers are more receptive to the new aesthetic values and perhaps defend them with excessive zeal, but older writers did the same thing in their day. Disagreements between generations are natural and productive, in his view.

In part the changes in tone discernible in the 1903 novel are due to the fact that Azorín has begun to resign himself to the limitations of the human condition and to derive what comfort he can from relativism and skepticism. Antonio reflects that in life there is nothing which is great or small, for a grain of sand can appear as a mountain to a simple man. Everything is relative to the individual and to his time. The gross error which Sarrió finds in one of his cookbooks and the erroneous newspaper account of his meeting with Antonio in Madrid demonstrate that books are fallacious and that falsehoods constantly pass for the truth. If man cannot even report the present correctly, he obviously cannot learn what happened in distant times and places. Since in reality we know nothing, we should acknowledge our incompetence and refrain from making judgments.

Antonio was first seen unpacking a suitcase which contained clothing and four volumes by Montaigne, one of the writers Azorín most admired. At the end of Part II the same articles are put back into the suitcase and Antonio departs for Madrid. In Part III he tells his own story in the first person. Using a variation of the technique found in the third section of *Will*, Antonio bares his soul in the five letters he writes to Pepita. In them he paints his life as a journalist, writing things he does not wish to write, reviewing books he cannot force himself to read, talking with people for whom he feels no esteem. He pours out his loneliness and nostalgia for the happier days spent in Petrel. For the first time his "dreadful spiritual torments" are actually made visible, and Antonio emerges as a clearly defined human being. "Here I lead a terrible life. . . . But it is necessary to be here, Pepita; it is necessary to live in this horrible Madrid; in the provinces one cannot win fame" (I, 1110-11). Despite his efforts, fame eludes him. Even worse, he feels that his personality is disintegrating.

In Part III Antonio visits Torrijos and Infantes. The chapters describing these towns are the most explicitly *noventayochista* ones of the book in their portrayal of socioeconomic decay and their call for reform. Torrijos is the prototype of the dead towns of Castile. An archaic mentality prevails and the peasants obstinately cling to old ways. Infantes is equally depressing. Its old mansions are empty and crumbling. The history of the town is presented as that of all Spain, brought to its present ruin by the policies initiated under Philip II and by Spanish Catholicism, "gloomy, aggressive, intolerant" (I, 1152). The cure for this prostration and melancholy is economic progress. The people must be assured of a decent existence so that they can believe that there is more to life than resignation and sorrow.

The world of *Antonio Azorín* is as silent as was that of *Will*. Antonio and Verdú chat fragmentarily from time to time. "Long silences interrupt their colloquies" (I, 1070). Antonio and a cleric stroll through the countryside and exchange an occasional word. With its fables, sketches of the lives of anonymous figures, and observations on the plant and insect world, *Antonio Azorín* is more digressive than the preceding novel. Descriptions of landscapes and interiors are extremely detailed, whereas those of human figures are very brief. Rather than analyze his characters, Azorín prefers to suggest certain of their traits. He pictures a number of them as representative figures, less as individuals than as members of some class or group. An old man who sells heraldic cards is one of those people who pass through or live in the towns of Spain but are ignored by novelists. This "one of those" technique is not limited to episodic figures. Verdú is "a beautiful example... of one of those men who gesticulate easily, who walk rapidly, who speak tumultuously" (I, 1070). In effect, the reader is expected to draw on his own knowledge of human nature to fill in the outline of these characters. As in *Will*, characters are often compared to paintings. A servant reminds Antonio of a Flemish genre painting. Pepita and her sisters resemble women painted by the Renaissance artists Raphael and Ghirlandaio. These pictorial allusions have an evocative power, conjuring up an image which complements the few details given by Azorín.

In recent years several critics have maintained that parts of *Antonio Azorín* were written before *Will* and have minimized the differences between the two novels.[11] The similarities are indeed numerous, and in both novels Azorín explores many of the same problems, but ideological and stylistic differences do exist. The protagonist of *Antonio Azorín* displays a greater degree of tolerance. He is less disoriented. His literary vocation gives some sense of direction to his life. The epilogue of *Will* left Antonio in a dead-end situation, whereas in the last lines of *Antonio Azorín* he sits down at his desk and begins to write: "I tidy my papers: I moisten my pen. And I begin..." (I, 1159). Verdú and Sarrió offer a more positive example than did Yuste. The element of protest is still present, but toned down. Affective values gain in importance, as does the use of irony. And in *Antonio Azorín* there is a greater interest in scenes of daily existence and the lives of ordinary people, both of which are characteristic of future works. It is true, however, that neither Antonio nor his creator has yet worked out a balance between the active and the contemplative life; the man of reflection and the man of will are still in conflict.

III   Las confesiones de un pequeño filósofo
(The Confessions of a Little Philosopher)

The author of the final volume of the trilogy is ostensibly Antonio himself.[12] The book is introduced by J.M.R., who explains that when Antonio's friends learned that he was thinking of running for Parliament they managed to convince him that the political arena was not for him. Somewhat sadly, he agreed to write a book instead. The result is *Las confesiones de un pequeño filósofo* (The Confessions of a Little Philosopher, 1904).

The note of humility and modesty suggested by the word *pequeño* is reiterated in the first chapter, entitled, "Yo no sé si escribir..." (I Do Not Know Whether to Write...). On a peaceful summer night as Antonio sits in the library of the family's country house near Monóvar his childhood and adolescence appear before his eyes. He wonders if a little philosopher such as he, who lives on a grain of sand lost in infinity, should set down on paper the minuscule events of his prosaic life. Despite his hesitation he decides to proceed with an evocation of his past. In the second chapter, "Escribiré" (I Shall Write), he outlines the method he will follow. He has no intention of giving all the dry, meaningless facts (names, dates, titles of works) which are normally found in an autobiography. Rather, he will choose from among his recollections certain vivid, unconnected moments so as to communicate to the reader "an undulating, flexible, ingenuous sensation" (II, 38) of his life. In short, he will adhere to the novelistic formula recommended in *Will*: "fragments, separate sensations" (I, 864). Each chapter of *The Confessions* is a discrete unit, related to preceding or succeeding ones only in that all are a reflection of Antonio's sensibility.

The first two chapters establish Antonio as the protagonist-narrator and make clear the retrospective and introspective nature of the confessions which are to follow. We, the readers, are to be given a portrait of the artist as a young boy during the formative years spent in Monóvar and Yecla. In a number of chapters, scenes and people are presented as they appeared to the child. His first teacher looms over him and with "barbarous insistence" makes him go over his primer again and again until an exhausted Antonio breaks into sobs. This use of the "innocent eye" point of view creates an impression of artlessness and is effective in enlisting sympathy for the child. The narrator cultivates a special relationship with his readers, asking their indulgence for relating such trifling things and reminding them that they too were once young.

Turning to the past, Antonio searches for the roots of his present personality and traces the awakening of his sensibility. During the hours spent in the study hall of the school in Yecla he used to gaze out the windows. The view of the green fields was a remedy for his sorrows, and it instilled in him a love of nature. One night he visited the school observatory and looked at the moon through a telescope, and for the first time he experienced a feeling of "ineffable yearning" (II, 54). Antonio also finds that his preoccupation with the passage of time stems from his childhood, when he was often admonished for returning home late. This obsession with time is reflected in several chapters. The monster of "El monstruo y la vieja" (The Monster and the Old Woman) is the mechanical bird which keeps popping out of the cuckoo clock and marking the hours. It is a "symbol of the inexorable and of the eternal" (II, 75). Like the anemometer which ceaselessly spins, it is indifferent to the peasant whose crops have been destroyed or the suffering of the old woman begging alms. In the epilogue the adult Antonio returns to Yecla. He finds that the same atmosphere of inertia and resignation pervades the city, and as he and several old friends stroll about one of them utters the phrase which haunted Antonio as a boy: "It is already [too] late." On revisiting the school he detects some superficial changes, but the anemometer is still spinning away, indifferent to the joys and sorrows of men. When he sees a row of schoolboys file past he suddenly realizes, like Nietzsche, that "all is one and the same" (II, 94) and that his childhood emotions are being experienced by the current group of students.

A number of the chapters are sketches of Antonio's teachers in Yecla. Despite the strict program which the students were forced to follow, many of the professors seem to have been quite indulgent with their young charges. Antonio recalls with affection Father Peña, who calmly read his newspaper during French class and was unperturbed by Antonio's highly original translations. Father Joaquín, who had the audacity to read the liberal newspaper *El Imparcial*, was the object of the boy's profound veneration. Particularly charming is the sketch of Father Miranda, who was in the habit of dozing off in the midst of his own lectures on world history. The rumor that he is devouring the pigeons of the school's dovecote impresses his students far more than do the feats of Caesar or Hannibal. Equally heroic in the eyes of the younger boys is the student who visits the prostitute who lives near the school and since he has no money leaves his vest with her by way of payment.

In *The Confessions* Antonio cultivates the aesthetic potential of the commonplace. He confesses that unlike other boys he never longed to be a general or a bishop. His secret ambition was to be able to enter into the minds of ordinary people: shopkeepers, traveling entertainers, or candle makers. These *vidas opacas* (undistinguished, apparently gray lives) are for him as filled with meaning and value as are those of the men who figure in history books. In *The Confessions* the author is alert to the significance of things which are usually ignored. Objects are endowed with meaning and a life of their own. Antonio declares: "I love things: this concern for the essence of the things which surround us has been dominant in my life" (II, 86). He devotes a chapter to doors and another to windows, noting that the sight of certain windows can awaken in us an inexplicable feeling of disquietude. He realizes that if he were to try to pin down this feeling he would probably be unable to do so, because "the mystery of these windows lies in something vague, something latent, something like a presentiment, or like a recollection of we know not what…" (II, 84-85).

Attempting to communicate the sense of mystery he perceives in the world around him, the narrator often resorts to words such as "indefinable," "ineffable," "inexplicable," "unutterable." It is often what is not said, what is left deliberately vague that is most suggestive. In the final chapter of the first edition of *The Confessions* Antonio evokes the figure of María Rosario at age fifteen. The moment he would like to recapture is, significantly, one of silence. "I feel a secret anguish when I evoke this unique moment in our lives, a moment that will not return, María Rosario, when the two of us were face to face, gazing at one another without saying anything" (II, 88). That moment cannot be relived in a literal sense, but it can be recreated through memory and preserved through art.

One of the most obvious differences between *The Confessions* and the two preceding novels is the greater conciseness of the 1904 book. The extremely detailed descriptions of the first two volumes of the trilogy have disappeared. Azorín has now mastered the technique of the small, revealing detail which is capable of evoking an entire state of consciousness or the essence of an experience. The description of Yecla in *Will* told how the city looked, but Azorín tended to overwhelm the reader with a mass of details. The far briefer description in *The Confessions* captures the feel of the city and conveys a sense of how its atmosphere colors the lives of its inhabitants. Both the sounds (tolling of bells) and colors (gray, black, brown) are mournful ones. The greenness of the small fertile plain has the effect of making the surrounding grayness seem even more lugubrious. Antonio speaks of the congenital melancholy of the city which reaches its peak during Holy Week when images of a bloodstained Christ and a sorrowing Mary are paraded through the streets. In *The Confessions* it is the writer's sensibility rather than the narration of events which predominates, and he is as much poet as philosopher.

The little philosopher of *The Confessions* is far removed from the angry young man of *Will.* Antonio no longer bitterly denounces the ills of Spain or flies into a rage over the follies of mankind. Rather, he contemplates people, places, and things with quiet melancholy. Writing of the teachers at the school in Yecla, he names those for whom he felt affection. The anonymity of the others is preserved. He is still distressed by the submissiveness and inertia of the inhabitants of Yecla and by their joyless religiosity, but the element of protest is muted. Antonio's agreeing to write a book rather than a political manifesto is symbolic of Azorín's decision that contemplation rather than action is his forte.

Azorín was by nature reticent. In *Memories* he describes himself as a writer who never revealed his innermost feelings. In *The Confessions*, which is the most literally autobiographical of his novels, he insists that the personal experiences narrated are Antonio's. The fiction that Antonio is the author of the work is a transparent one, but it acts as a screen behind which Azorín is able to partially conceal himself. Moreover, Antonio's forthrightness is more apparent than real. His confessions focus on the years in Yecla. Very little is said about his early life in Monóvar and he is uncommunicative about his immediate family.[13]

IV Tomás Rueda

To a certain extent all Azorín's novels are autobiographical, although it is the 1902-1904 trilogy which is customarily so designated. In those works in which Azorín recreates other authors' characters, they too look at the world through his eyes and share his sensibility and obsessions. *Tomás Rueda*, originally published under the title *El licenciado Vidriera visto por Azorín* (1915), gives new life to the protagonist of Cervantes's exemplary novel *El licenciado Vidriera* (The Man of Glass), with the author remaking Tomás in his own image.[14] The external outline of Tomás's life is, of course, at variance with that of Azorín's, but the essence of the

two beings is similar. Tomás, a lonely, pensive child, markedly
resembles the protagonist of *The Confessions.*

Following his days as a student in Salamanca, Tomás leaves his
books behind and sets out to experience life directly, believing that
more can be learned from living than from reading. Azorín comments rather sadly that Tomás does not yet realize that having
sampled or left untasted all that the world has to offer will, when
he is old, cause equal regret. After having traveled widely, Tomás
returns to Salamanca and resumes his studies. Subsequently he
succumbs to the passion of love and, when he recovers, realizes
that he is no longer the same man. He now possesses greater clarity
of vision, but his heightened sensitivity occasions acute suffering,
for he is painfully aware of the irritations of daily life. Despite his
love for his country, he decides to leave Spain in search of a more
congenial and refined environment. The final chapter finds Tomás
in Flanders which, as described by Azorín, resembles the quiet,
orderly, restful world of a Vermeer painting. There he is accompanied by Gabriela, a character modeled on Azorín's wife. Her presence plus the inner reality which sustains Tomás enables him to
continue writing. One day there arrives from Spain a letter which
he reads with jubilation. The final words of the novel are "The
letter read thus..." ("La carta decía así..." [III, 331]). Tomás is the
receptacle into which Azorín has poured the distillate of his own
life: the child's solemnity and wonder, the youth's uncertainty as to
whether to pursue an active or contemplative existence, the adult's
hypersensitivity and dissatisfaction with Spain, the writer's need
for a sustaining illusion.[15]

In *Tomás Rueda* the substance of the story is found between the
lines, in what is merely implied. The circumstantial accuracy of
the descriptions of setting in *Will* and *Antonio Azorín* would be
inappropriate here, for external details are not important. The
first chapter, for instance, does not offer a room-by-room tour of
the house, because it is not the house but the sense of its strange-
ness which is significant. Rather than jarring the reader with a
crude recital of bald facts—the child's mother has died, his father
is bankrupt, and the furnishings of the house are being sold—it is
left to him to infer what has happened. It is as if this part of the
story were being filtered through the uncomprehending mind of
the child, a mind which does not perceive the reason for the
father's sudden rages and furious arguments with "other gentlemen"—his creditors—or for the inexplicable disappearance of the

mother's writing desk, tapestries, and cartloads of books. The adult world of financial ruin lies beyond the realm of the child's experience, and the events of that world, seen through his eyes, appear shrouded in mystery. This sense of mystery which is a tangible presence throughout the book is especially pronounced in the closing phrase, which leaves the story of Tomás suspended in midair.

Azorín devoted the years immediately preceding the composition of *Tomás Rueda* to a study of the classics of Spanish literature, seeking to inspire in his countrymen an appreciation of their cultural heritage and an awareness of what they have in common with their predecessors. A similar intent underlies *Tomás Rueda*, where Azorín demonstrates that the emotions of a seventeenth-century Spaniard are basically no different from those of a twentieth-century one. To develop the theme of the spiritual unity between past and present and ensure that the modern reader will at all times sympathize with Tomás, Azorín has chosen a narrator whose relation to the story changes. At first he appears in the role of storyteller, facing his audience and speaking directly to it. Later he appears as the author of the story, transmitting his material in writing rather than orally. In both cases he surveys the narrative from a dual vantage point in time, that of the seventeenth and that of the twentieth century.

The postface of the 1915 edition indicates that *Tomás Rueda* began as a story for children.[16] Whatever the original intention, Azorín must soon have realized that his tale was not the type to appeal to youthful readers. *Tomás Rueda* is a story for adults which is told, in part, as if it were intended for children. The opening "Once upon a time" immediately transports us back to the world of childhood. The narrator begins by suggesting several possible subjects to see which of them will evoke a response from his audience. It apparently fails to react favorably to the suggestions of a tale about a king, a great nobleman, or a valiant captain, and so he settles on the idea of a tale about a child.

The narrator proceeds at a leisurely pace, slowly creating the atmosphere which has molded the character and sensibility of the boy. The impression that the story is being told orally is strengthened by his informal, conversational style. He frequently corrects himself, modifying or clarifying a remark he has made or adding a detail he had forgotten to include earlier. On occasion he digresses slightly and subsequently has trouble recollecting his original train of thought. At other times he stops to address a few parenthetical remarks to his public and then, realizing he has become sidetracked, says, "But let us continue with our tale" (III, 284). By speaking directly to his listeners, asking them questions, consulting them, he draws them into the story and makes them feel they are personally participating in it. During these first chapters the storyteller adapts his method of narration, language, and style to his subject and to his imaginary audience. It is essential that the reader identify with Tomás and see the world through his eyes. To do this, he must himself become a child again, and this is what the narrator encourages him to do. In his role as storyteller he creates a magic circle into which the reader is drawn. Once inside that circle, the reader lays aside his sense of adult superiority.

In the fifth chapter, "Acaba la aurora" (Dawn Ends), Tomás's childhood comes to a close. The change in his life is paralleled by a change in the narrator's relationship to his character. In the first section of the chapter Tomás is still "our youngster," "our child"; in the third section he becomes "our character," "our friend." Narrator and character are fast becoming contemporaries, and this necessitates a change in the former's method of presentation. The storyteller is replaced by the author, and the imaginary listeners become adult readers. In Chapter 11, for instance, the author alerts his readers to the fact that they must now pay special attention if they are to perceive the subtle change that has come over Tomás ("Ah, dear readers! We are now reaching the most delicate part of this tale" [III, 320]) and mentions that "in a preceding chapter we have quoted the words of Hernán Pérez de Oliva" (III, 321). The story of Tomás's life is now obviously being conveyed in writing rather than orally.

The narrator is at one and the same time in the twentieth and in the seventeenth century. The story is organized around an axis, the two poles of which are past (*antes*) and present (*ahora*). But these poles constantly shift as the distance between them alternately expands and contracts. At times they are separated by three centuries, at other times by only a few months. In one of the sections of Chapter 4 the *antes* and the *ahora* refer respectively to the seventeenth and the twentieth century. In Chapter 1, by contrast, there is a very short span of time between the *antes* when Tomás's mother was still alive and the *ahora* of the child's present situation. As the years go by and "our child" becomes "our character,"

the child's *ahora* becomes the adult's *antes*. The narrator moves
freely between present and past, and at any point in his account
he can make the past more vivid by changing to the present tense
and depicting immediate scenes which make the reader feel he is
an eyewitness to events as they unfold. Certain experiences of
great intensity are thus portrayed in high relief. Chapter 6 begins
with the indication that eight years have elapsed since we last saw
Tomás. The narrator then wonders aloud how those years have
affected Tomás, and suddenly he, Tomás, and the reader are all in
Salamanca contemplating the almost imperceptible changes of
light and shadow on the white wall visible from Tomás's window.
As a result of the constant shifting of temporal planes, the past is so
woven into the present that the distinction between the two melts
away.

Azorín has transmitted the story of Tomás Rueda with impres-
sive skill. The changes in Tomás's life have been paralleled by
changes in the narrator's relationship to the character, enabling
the reader to identify with Tomás and share his feelings. By sur-
veying the story from a shifting perspective in time, Azorín has
been able to underline the spiritual continuity between past and
present. *Tomás Rueda* is, justifiably, one of his most praised
works.[17]

V Don Juan

The traditional image of Don Juan is that of the libertine who
dashes from one seduction to the next, the man of passion and
daring who defies the laws of man and of God. Considering
Azorín's predilections, it is not surprising to find that his Don Juan
bears little resemblance to the dynamic, mythic figure of earlier
literature. In the prologue to his novel Azorín quickly disposes of
Don Juan's past and lays the ground for a new interpretation of
him. Don Juan del Prado y Ramos once was a great sinner, to be
sure, but a serious illness has left him transformed. His case, suggests Azorín, is not without parallel, for the thirteenth-century
poet Gonzalo de Berceo related the story of a lascivious monk who
was first denied entry into heaven but, on the intervention of the
Virgin Mary, was given a second chance. Returning to earth, he
led a life which assured him of salvation.

The narrative thread of *Don Juan* (1922) is so tenuous as to be
practically nonexistent. Not only is the action minimal; it is presented obliquely. We are given not deeds but their repercussions,

not conversations but their echoes, and we are required to be alert
to the implications of word and gesture. The first two chapters
inform us of the essential traits of the protagonist. Don Juan's life
appears to be governed by the principle of moderation in all things
and a desire to atone for his past excesses. He is swift to help those
in need, often doing so anonymously, and is forgiving of others'
faults. He is moved by beauty and has a strong sense of justice. We
have here a spiritualized, altruistic Don Juan who has wearied of
worldly delights and is no longer a devotee of Eros.

The small city where he resides is conducive to meditation.
With its Roman bridge and ruined walls, Gothic cathedral, and
Renaissance town hall, it has an aura of majesty and repose. The
past has left its imprint on the present in the form of a "spiritual
sediment" (IV, 223), and in the market vendors wrap their wares
in the leaves of old books and papers dating from the seventeenth
century. The atmosphere of the city is epitomized by the colors
white and blue: the white and blue wall of a tiny patio on a
deserted street, the dazzling whiteness of the Capuchin convent
set beneath the blueness of the sky. Little of note has happened
here, but Azorín relates one episode which has a bearing on the
present. In the sixteenth century there was an epic battle between
the nuns of the order of Saint Jerome and a bishop who was
determined to restrict their freedom and impose a more ascetic life
upon them. The bishop was only partially successful. A degree of
laxity still persists in the prosperous Hieronymite convent, and its
current abbess, Sor Natividad, has about her a faint air of sensuality which Don Juan finds attractive.

Once Azorín has sketched the outlines of his protagonist and the
spirit of the city (Chapters 1 to 10), he provides glimpses of various
people with whom Don Juan is acquainted. One of the most important of these is the teacher who wants his pupils to remember
their school days with pleasure. His classroom is decorated with
pictures of animals and trees instead of the garish illustrations of
Biblical scenes which haunted Antonio Azorín. The schoolmaster
takes his students to visit local craftsmen and into the country to
study nature. The children return from these excursions carrying
armfuls of flowers, singing and laughing. Their education is very
different from that received by Antonio.

The fact that Don Juan, the former transgressor of all laws, is
now deeply concerned with justice is suggested in the next four
chapters. In the first of these a pompous magistrate takes to task a

young man, Pozas, for making a distinction between what is just
and what is legal. According to the magistrate, Pozas's ideas are
outrageous and would subvert the very foundations of society.
(Given the elliptical technique of the novel, we never learn precisely what Pozas is advocating.) The conflict between justice and
the law is further illustrated in incidents involving two governors.
The first governor is a poet, appalled by the wretched conditions
of the local orphanage, who attempts to do something to amelio-
rate the plight of the emaciated, ragged children. He promptly
runs afoul of the law, is removed from office, and is publicly
censured for being out of touch with reality. His replacement lives
by the letter of the law. When Don Juan and Pozas request that a
group of prisoners be treated in a more humane fashion, the governor cites the legislation which prohibits this. Since the authori-
ties are only interested in legality, Don Juan undertakes to remedy
injustice and comfort the distressed whenever feasible. His humanitarianism is best exemplified in his encounter with a barefoot
child staggering along under a load of firewood. Don Juan seats
the child on his knees and cleanses his bleeding feet. Two weeks
later the city receives a large gift of money to be spent on the
building of magnificent schools with special facilities for the care
of poor children. While the mayor delivers a speech in praise of
the mysterious donor, Don Juan stands amidst the crowd, smiling.

Having shown Don Juan's philanthropy and concern for justice,
Azorín turns to a third trait pointed out in the initial description of
the character, the attraction which beauty holds for him. Sor
Natividad and her coquettish niece Jeannette represent, respectively, a "celestial" and a "terrible" temptation for Don Juan. He
does not, however, succumb, and the epilogue of the book finds
him converted into Brother Juan. He explains to an interlocutor
that he now knows the highest form of love: *piedad* (compassion,
piety). As he speaks, a dove flies across the blue sky.

None of Azorín's novels is complete without at least some reference to time. In *Don Juan*, Jeannette's father, Don Gonzalo, is a
collector of Roman coins and those coins, which have survived the
passing of the civilization which minted them, stand as a symbol
of permanence. They have passed from hand to hand, generation
after generation, and are still intact. Don Gonzalo also observes
that historians write about great men, not realizing that without
the intervention of such men the course of history would have
been exactly the same. With the deliberate imprecision which is

characteristic of *Don Juan* we are left in ignorance of the age of
the protagonist, but the autumnal tone of the novel suggests an
aging Don Juan. The passing of time has brought him to a recognition of the vanity of earthly riches. In 1920 Azorín wrote that
spirit, not matter, moves the world and that what is usually re-
puted to be evanescent is what is truly imperishable. Love, solidarity, and justice are superior to inexorable nature (IV, 212-13).
That profession of faith is echoed in *Don Juan*.[18]

VI   Doña Inés

In 1925 Azorín again turns to the literature of the past for
inspiration and finds in José Zorrilla's Romantic drama *Don Juan
Tenorio* a figure worthy of a different role. The story of Azorín's
Doña Inés de Silva begins in Madrid in 1840. After Don Juan
abruptly terminates their affair she returns to her childhood home
in Segovia. There she relives the experiences of her fifteenth-
century ancestor Doña Beatriz, falling in love with a blue-eyed,
golden-haired poet, Diego Lodares, who is much younger than
she. It is in *Doña Inés* that Azorín most fully elaborates the concept of eternal recurrence. On the thematic level the concept is
developed through the technique of the story-within-a-story. On
the structural level it is exemplified in a series of parallel chapters
and a complex system of recurring motifs. Stylistically it is expressed through repetition and the use of reflected images.[19]

Doña Inés's uncle, Don Pablo, is engaged in writing a biography of Doña Beatriz. Over a period of several days he recounts to
his niece the story of Beatriz, her husband Don Esteban de Silva,
and Guillén de Treceño, a youthful, blue-eyed, golden-haired
troubadour.[20] Prior to the appearance of the troubadour, Doña
Beatriz has never known real love, for her husband is a violent
man of action and therefore lacking in sensibility. When he learns
of his wife's infidelity he murders her paramour, and Doña Beatriz
loses her mind. Doña Inés is at first only mildly interested in Don
Pablo's narrative, which is spun out over Chapters 30 to 33, but as
the similarity between her situation and that of Doña Beatriz
becomes apparent, her interest becomes obsessive. Every time
Don Pablo strays from the point and starts talking about men of
action she anxiously interrupts with the phrase "And the troubadour?" This refrain is repeated throughout Chapter 32. In Chapter 33 Doña Inés's increasing identification with Doña Beatriz is

likewise conveyed through the device of a refrain. Six times she interrupts her uncle, first repeating his last words, then saying she does not wish to hear any more, and then quickly asking, "What happened next?"

In succeeding chapters Doña Inés's feeling of identification with her ancestor becomes so complete that she wonders whether she is Inés or a reincarnation of Beatriz and whether time really exists. This last question is the motif which runs through Chapters 35 to 37. Standing before the recumbent statue atop Doña Beatriz's tomb in the cathedral, Doña Inés's confusion reaches its height and she no longer knows who or where she is. While in this hallucinatory state she hears her name whispered. Turning, she is embraced by Diego. From this point on the two stories diverge. Fearful of discovering the first sign of indifference in her young poet, Doña Inés embarks for Argentina where she establishes a school for the children of poor Spaniards. She is last seen at the window of the room to which she is now confined, suffering— appropriately—from heart trouble. And in the garden below her window there is perhaps among the children one who is seated in the shade of an *ombú* tree. Thus as one cycle is ending another is beginning, for as a child Diego lived in Argentina and spent his days reading beneath an *ombú*, the tree which "symbolizes the poetic and sentimental tradition of the gaucho" (IV, 776) and "defies time" (IV, 846).

Through the device of the story-within-a-story Azorín has illustrated that in the endlessly repeated cycle of the universe "everything, in different form, will everlastingly be renewed" ("todo, siendo distinto, volverá perdurablemente a renovarse" [II, 724]). Although he does not belabor the point, the parallels between the two stories are numerous. Both bear the subtitle *Historia de amor* (Love Story). The important characters in Azorín's *Doña Inés* have their counterpart in Don Pablo's *Doña Beatriz*. The similarity between the two heroines is pronounced. Both are of high station, physically similar and, as Azorín gracefully puts it, "in the autumn of life." Both become enamored of a much younger man, and for both this love is apparently a new experience. Doña Beatriz's final madness is momentarily echoed in the cathedral scene when Inés briefly loses all sense of reality. Likewise, there is a physical resemblance between the two poets. Both are shadowy, purely passive figures. There is also, perhaps, an implicit analogy between the insensitive man of action Don Esteban and Don Juan.

Furthermore, there is a parallel or spiritual kinship between the two "authors." Don Pablo, one of Azorín's most strongly autobiographical characters, frequents libraries and archives and has a passion for books. A contemplative man of sensibility rather than of action, he tries to avoid intense emotions which would disturb the serenity which enables him to enjoy a silent communication with the world around him and which is essential to his creativity. He is acutely sensitive to time and lives as much in the past as in the present. Possessed of a prodigious memory of sensations, a voice or a sound unexpectedly makes him relive with distressing exactness a sensation experienced years before.[21] This is as painful for him as the fact that he sees the future in the present. Witnessing a minor contretemps he has a presentiment of dire consequences. The face of a sick child allows him to glimpse the specter of death. Having read that the German writer E.T.A. Hoffmann suffered from similar apprehensions, Don Pablo has labeled this ailment "Hoffmann's disease." Azorín too is afflicted with this malady.[22]

The artist who seeks to escape the temporality to which man is condemned can do so by transcending time and contemplating life from a divine or supratemporal perspective. In *Doña Inés* it is Don Pablo who is permitted to glimpse this perspective. El Eterno (The Eternal One) appears to him in a dream and shows him a sight He allows few mortals to see. Lifting His arm on high, He lets a handful of sand slip from between His fingers. Each of the grains is a world, and the two or three seconds it has taken for that handful of worlds to fall represent man's thousands and thousands of centuries. The Lord explains that because of his limited intelligence man is unable to conceive a universe different from the one he inhabits, but He can create thousands of universes in which there would be neither life nor death, neither unity nor diversity. He stresses that the most man can do is comprehend the possibility of the existence of such universes. But Azorín, struggling to escape the tyranny of time, tries to do more than this. The novels of the following period are attempts to create his own timeless worlds. The chapter in which Don Pablo recounts his dream occupies a key position in the novel. It immediately follows the story of Doña Beatriz and in turn is followed by the three chapters in which the existence of time is questioned. The repeated raising of that question indicates that while Azorín was developing the concept of eternal recurrence he was already beginning to search for other solutions.

The concept of recurrence which is the main theme of *Doña Inés* is expressed on the structural level by a series of parallel chapters or groups of chapters and by a network of recurring motifs. Upon her return to Segovia, Doña Inés immediately goes to pay her respects to her aunt and uncle. Three chapters are devoted to the presentation of each character. Tía Pompilia, one of Azorín's most vivid creations, is a whirlwind of activity. Fearful of immobility, she goes precipitately from room to room, constantly rearranges the furniture, and impatiently complains of her servants' slowness. Whereas she is portrayed in constant movement, Don Pablo is seen standing as if posed for a portrait. He cannot bear to see the furniture shifted even one centimeter, and silence reigns in his apartment. There is, however, one important similarity within the two sets of chapters. Both relatives ask Inés if she has already heard of Diego, refer to his talent, and assure their niece that she will soon meet him.

In the next block of parallel chapters—23 to 28—Inés and Diego are slowly drawn together. The correspondences between the two culminating chapters of this block are so numerous that the chapters are almost duplicates. They also occur simultaneously rather than successively. Each consists of one long paragraph. Doña Inés and Diego, in their respective rooms, gaze at the evening star and think similar thoughts. She reflects on lost youth and love, he on poetry and love. The obsessive desire felt by the two characters is so intense that it acts as a magnet, irresistibly pulling them together until in the cathedral scene Doña Inés is indeed embraced by the young poet.

The repercussions of their kiss extend throughout the city, which is turned topsy-turvy. A miser gives alms. Weather vanes revolve madly. Doors slam. Rumors zigzag and whirl through the streets. Faced with such a scandalous situation, both the spiritual and temporal powers of the city feel compelled to intervene. Two chapters are devoted to the ecclesiastical authority and two to the secular. With consummate discretion the bishop suggests to his friend Don Pablo that an absorption with the past may blind us to present realities which demand our attention; in other words, Don Pablo should do something about his wayward niece. The provincial governor delivers an equally indirect admonition to Diego.

Thus the main points of the Inés-Diego story are presented in parallel chapters. Inés visits her aunt and uncle and twice hears the poet's praises sung. She strolls through the city and is gradually drawn to the Alcázar, where she and Diego contemplate the same landscape, then turn and gaze into each other's eyes. She dreams of Diego while he dreams of her. In the cathedral they embrace and again gaze into each other's eyes. Finally Church and State administer two extremely subtle rebukes. At that point Inés learns of her servant Plácida's love for Diego. That discovery and the reflection that initial ardor inevitably cools determine her departure for the New World.

Doña Inés is a tightly constructed work. The more it is examined the more apparent becomes the closeness of the delicate webbing which supports it. In the first seven chapters, for instance, the only thing that actually "happens" is that Doña Inés receives a letter, but the story which begins with her return to Segovia in Chapter 8 would be incomplete without the foundation which is laid in these preliminary pages. Here is created the atmosphere necessary to that story and the pressure of time begins to be felt. The circle which will be closed in the final chapter begins to be traced, and certain motifs which will recur throughout the book are introduced. In the room where Doña Inés and Don Juan meet there hangs a yellowed lithograph which portrays the city of Buenos Aires and its environs. Whenever Doña Inés enters the room her eyes are drawn to the print. The significance of this attraction becomes apparent later when it is revealed that as a child Diego lived near Buenos Aires and that Doña Inés ends her days in Argentina. A line is thus drawn linking the beginning and end of the novel. During this first section attention is repeatedly focused on Doña Inés's hands, seen testing the firmness of her skin, trying to smooth away wrinkles, holding the letter sent by Don Juan, crumpling the letter, and, finally, clutching the gold coins which cannot buy back her lost youth. The image of her hands acts as a thread which binds these chapters together.[23] Variations upon the gold-time motif are found in the final chapter of the Doña Beatriz story, which is framed by references to the golden stream of sand of the hourglass on Don Pablo's desk, and in Chapter 34, where the brevity of human existence and the relativity of time are symbolized by the grains of sand which fall from the divine hand.

The concept of eternal recurrence is further illustrated through repetition and reflection. The repetition of images and phrases, even of entire sentences, is the perfect stylistic equivalent of the idea of *eterno retorno*. Mention has already been made of how

Doña Inés repeatedly interrupts Don Pablo's narrative with the question "And the troubadour?" Similarly in "Aquelarre en Segovia" (Witches' Sabbath in Segovia) four old women whisper the same piece of gossip in Tía Pompilia's ear. Four times she replies, "I already knew that!" This entire chapter is one of fourfold repetition. It begins with four ominous phrases: "Dark clouds. Noise of sieves. Spider on mirror. Overturned saltshaker" (IV, 817). Four old women set out from the four corners of Segovia. As each advances through her quadrant of the city a building is seen in the background: the cathedral, a portion of the aqueduct, the seminary, or the Alcázar. Each of the witchlike figures proceeds at the same pace. Each pauses and utters a few words. The four finally converge on the house of Tía Pompilia, deliver their "news," bang their staffs on the floor, and file back to their respective corners. Again, the same four buildings are framed at the end of the four streets along which the four "witches" retrace their steps.

Even more effective than the repetition of words or phrases is the use of variations on a theme, as in Chapter 33, where Doña Inés repeatedly interrupts her uncle, in each instance using different words to express the same anxiety.[24] This technique is used again in the two "Obsession" chapters. Azorín thus illustrates the gist of the concept of eternal recurrence, the idea that unchanging essence is expressed in ever-changing form, that there is identity within variety. This last concept is also expressed through the use of reflected images. The original point of departure is Zorrilla's Doña Inés. She is freely recreated in Azorín's Doña Inés, who is a "reincarnation" of Doña Beatriz. There is a further series of mirrored images. Doña Inés is caught in a fading daguerreotype and in a portrait which has been painted of her, wherein she bears a striking resemblance to Doña Beatriz. In Chapter 7 her image is reflected in a mirror. In the final chapter her face is seen through a window. Each of the last four images of her is different and yet the same. This technique is used on every level of the novel, for Don Pablo is—figuratively speaking—a reflection of Azorín, just as Diego is a reflection of Guillén, who is in turn a reflection of the fifteenth-century troubadour Macías el Enamorado.[25]

In *Doña Inés*, one of Azorín's finest works, the concept of eternal recurrence constitutes the form and substance of the novel. Thematically the concept is expressed in a timeless love story played out before the same backdrop in two different centuries. The closing lines of the novel hint that a new actor is already in the wings preparing to step into the role of the poet. On the structural level, the concept of recurrence is exemplified in parallel chapters and a series of motifs which weave in and out, linking chapters and groups of chapters. Stylistically, the governing principle is that of unchanging content expressed in ever-changing form. The same ideas and emotions are clothed in different words. The same characters are caught in different poses, framed or reflected in different mirrors. Every aspect of the novel illustrates the idea that "everything changes in appearance and is repeated in essence through the ages" (I, 888). This cyclical theory of time provides for permanence and duration despite the endless flux visible in the world of man, and it partially alleviates the pain caused by the inexorable passage of time.

CHAPTER 4

Success and Maturity:
II. Essays and Sketches

FOLLOWING the completion of the three novels dealing with his alter ego Antonio, Azorín turned to a concentrated scrutiny of Spain. Between 1905 and 1915 appeared his most famous studies of its life and literature, people and landscape. In *Los pueblos* (Towns, 1905), *La ruta de Don Quijote* (The Route of Don Quixote, 1905), *España* (Spain, 1909), and *Castilla* (Castile, 1912), which consist of sketches of provincial life, descriptions of the countryside, and evocations of the past, he focuses on what is for him the essence of his homeland. Believing that "the great writers of a country are its very spirit" (II, 921), he also endeavors to educate his countrymen on the subject of their literary tradition. The four major volumes of essays published between 1912 and 1915—*Lecturas españolas* (Spanish Readings, 1912), *Clásicos y modernos* (Classic and Modern Authors, 1913), *Los valores literarios* (Literary Values, 1914), and *Al margen de los clásicos* (Marginal Notes on the Classics, 1915)—reveal the essential characteristics of his work as a literary critic. The essays range from expository ones, in which Azorín presents the main ideas of an author or book, to the lyrical comments and evocative recreations which predominate in *Marginal Notes*.

The 1905 to 1915 decade is a high point in Azorín's career. During the ensuing years there is a noticeable decline in his zeal as a reformer and in his vigor as a critic of Spain, and he becomes increasingly detached from present reality.[1] *Una hora de España (Entre 1560 y 1590)* (An Hour in the Life of Spain [Between 1560 and 1590]) represents his almost total reconciliation with the Spanish tradition. In this work, the text of the address he read on entering the Royal Spanish Academy in 1924, Azorín declares that his intention is to understand, not to judge, the past, and that sincere affection, respect, and tolerance are essential to such an undertaking. He now defends many of the things he had formerly attacked. With reference to the decadence of Spain, a major concern of earlier essays and novels, he asserts that it is time to set the record straight: "Let us react against this idea. Such decadence has not existed" (IV, 565).[2] In support of this startling claim, he argues that a country that has discovered and colonized a new world cannot be termed decadent. He also insists that it is absurd to criticize Spain for its scientific infecundity, for as a profoundly Christian nation Spain was more interested in the pursuit of virtue than in intellectual speculation.

An article published in 1905,[3] "Proceso psicológico" (Psychological Process), sheds light on the reasons for the evolution of Azorín's attitude toward the Spanish tradition. Here he describes a supposedly hypothetical individual who is reared in a strongly religious family and who, during his adolescence, begins to read the great writers of his country. At the university this individual finds himself plunged into an impersonal setting which offers instruction but not education, and he follows his own impulses, becoming intensely individualistic and egotistic. These qualities impregnate his first works, in which he breaks with all established values. But as time passes and he encounters adversity in the literary world, he turns from the present and immerses himself in the study of the past. This study reinforces the spirit of traditionalism of his early education and upbringing, and he realizes that "the present, the life that we now live, is intimately bound to the past, is in fact its continuation" (VII, 403). He proceeds to examine the manifestations of this continuity: the old cities, monuments, and landscape of his country, and the silent, daily life of his fellow citizens. The tangible results of his observations are those books and articles in which he presents the national spirit. More profound is the psychological result, for his former egotism and individualism vanish and he feels himself part of the surrounding social, moral, and physical environment. He then perceives the strength of the roots which bind him to the tradition, art, beliefs, and ideals which have formed his nation.[4]

I   Los pueblos *(Towns)*

When *Los pueblos* (Towns) was published in 1905, Azorín

wrote an article in which he outlined the premise underlying these "essays on provincial life."[5] He insists that in the eyes of an observant person there is nothing in life which is insignificant or commonplace:

If you affirm that this town is gray and wander through it with an air of overwhelming superiority, I must tell you that the commonness and monotony lie not in the town, but in you. . . .Everything has its aesthetic and psychological value; the minute harmonies of things are as interesting for the psychologist and the artist as are the great universal syntheses. There is a new beauty, a new art in the small, in the insignificant details, as in the ordinary and the prosaic. The abstract and epic topics which until now poets have bandied about no longer say anything to us; it is no longer possible to speak in emphatic generalities about the countryside, Nature, love, or men; we need tiny occurrences which will reveal what life is like and which, harmoniously assembled, with simplicity, with clarity, will show us the mysterious force of the universe. (II, 237-38)

This same article contains several references to Montaigne who, along with Schopenhauer and Nietzsche, exerted a considerable influence on Azorín's early intellectual development. Montaigne's skepticism and pursuit of self-knowledge served as an example for Azorín, and in the French writer's *Essays* he found corroboration of his own views on education, love, and marriage and an interest in the concrete and prosaic.[6] "Montaigne is not a philosopher of the abstract, the confused, the obscure, the unintelligible, the inscrutable, the fantastic; Montaigne is a philosopher of the concrete, the minute, the trivial, the prosaic detail, what we see and touch every day at home and in the street" (VII, 229-30). Furthermore, Montaigne's personal, discursive style delighted Azorín, whose own essays are also of the informal or familiar type in which the author's personality plays an important role. They are not impersonal, learned treatises but sketches.

Since the short sketch is the basic unit of almost all Azorín's work, the distinction between his novels and his collections of essays is often a fine one. His description of *Tomás Rueda* as a "novelistic essay" underscores this blurring or overlapping of different literary forms. Frequently, *Towns* is reminiscent of *The Confessions of a Little Philosopher*. Both works are anecdotal, emphasize minutiae, and are characterized by simplicity of expression, understatement, and an air of informality. In both Azorín uses a technique similar to that of a poet writing a ballad and repeats phrases or entire sentences. An effect comparable to that of the fade-out in the cinema is created through the use of suspension points. Sketches trail off into thin air. In "La muerte de un amigo: Sarrió" (The Death of a Friend: Sarrió) the sentence "All passes away; people we have loved disappear from our side; a wake of love and melancholy remains in our spirit" appears near the beginning, at the midpoint, and at the end of the sketch, with suspension points being added in the last instance.[7] The use of the word *estela*, referring to the wake of a ship or the trail of a heavenly body, adds to the suggestiveness of the refrain.

Beginning the first sketch dealing with Sarrió, Azorín shares a sad piece of news with his readers. "The friends and admirers of the illustrious man will be filled with consternation when they read these lines. Sarrió is ill; Sarrió is disappearing..." (II, 111). Azorín reminds his readers that in the towns of Spain there are ordinary, insignificant beings who have charmed us with their affability and their simple words, beings whose disappearance grieves us as greatly as that of a great artist. There are beings, such as Sarrió, who have seen their world collapse about them and who during a period of years linger on, gradually losing all interest in life. Azorín then relates how upon going to visit his old friend he finds that Pepita is dead and her two sisters married. The house is now silent and the furniture covered with dust. When Sarrió appears, unshaven and carelessly dressed, he fails to recognize his former companion. Azorín silently departs. As he walks back through the town square he hears the chimes of the old clock which "marks its hours, rhythmic, eternal, indifferent to the sorrows of man..." (II, 116). Later, when he receives the telegram announcing Sarrió's death, he closes his eyes and recalls his friend's last trip to Madrid—recounted in *Antonio Azorín*—and adds several new details, such as Sarrió's disillusionment on finding that the filling of some bonbons he had bought did not correspond to the fraudulent labels. It is these small things, he asserts, which made Sarrió unique and memorable, even though the world was oblivious of his existence.

Several sketches are Cervantine in flavor. One of Azorín's own favorites was "El buen juez" (The Good Judge). During 1904 a translation of the judicial decisions of the French jurist Paul Magnaud was published in Spain. Instead of a standard book review, Azorín writes a fanciful story of how a copy of the book reaches the hands of a judge in a small town of La Mancha. The judge is of the same age and build as Don Quixote and is also named Alonso. After reading the book Don Alonso renders a decision which is just but without legal precedent, thereby creating a stir among his colleagues and friends. The good judge explains that justice is such a rarity that, when it does appear on earth, it leaves mortals astonished. Several passages in the sketch are an imitation of the style of *Don Quixote*, which is one of the books in Don Alonso's library.

Signs of change in Azorín's attitude toward certain aspects of the past of Spain are apparent in "Un hidalgo" (A Hidalgo), subtitled "Las raíces de España (The Roots of Spain). He sees in the punctilious, starving hidalgo of the picaresque novel *Lazarillo de Tormes* not false pride and sham but fortitude and suffering, concealed beneath an appearance of serenity. The hidalgo's sword symbolizes Spanish values: integrity, valor, dignity, and audacity. His house may be without furniture and his larder empty, but he accepts his fate with nobility and displays "legendary Spanish courtesy" (II, 178). Nostalgia for the past also informs "Una elegía" (An Elegy). It is a lament for the death of a sensitive, dreamy, melancholy young woman. Even more, it is a lament for a threatened way of life. Azorín again voices his affection for those age-old trades which are plied in the villages of Spain. The workshops of wheelwrights, harness makers, pewterers, and blacksmiths fascinate him, and he regrets the passing of these artisans who take pride in their work. Mass-produced articles, he reflects, cannot compare in durability or beauty with handcrafted pieces.

This last sketch is an excellent example of the reaction against industrial civilization which is reflected in turn-of-the-century European literature and art. The late-nineteenth-century faith in progress—apparent in Azorín's earliest works—soon gave way to a dissatisfaction with modern industrialized society.[8] This dissatisfaction is expressed in various ways in Azorín's writing. We have seen how he exalts the skills of humble craftsmen. His fascination with objects of daily domestic use is evident in his descriptions of interiors, where he pays special attention to kitchen utensils, pots, and water jugs which have been made by anonymous artists and which represent ties with the past. His portrayal of *vidas opacas*, his curiosity about the lives of small shopkeepers, and his concern for the peasantry are all part of his interest in the common people. They represent for him the real Spain. He celebrates the simple,

traditional way of life of small cities or towns. The very title
Towns is indicative of Azorín's preferences. This work speaks of his
love for the narrow, twisting, uneven streets of old Spanish cities
as opposed to the broad, straight avenues of the world's large
capitals. In *Will* Yuste laments the exodus of the peasants from the
land, and Antonio views Madrid as a nightmare city of chaos and
inhumanity. A new poetic feeling for nature is apparent in Azorín's
landscape descriptions. And his interest in the Middle Ages, seen
as an era of spontaneity and simplicity, is reflected in his love for
medieval cities and his eulogies of Berceo, Juan Ruiz, and the
ballad literature of Spain.

The little philosopher's gentle melancholy and his preoccupation with the passage of time are displayed in "La fiesta" (The
Fiesta). The protagonist is an elderly, blind poet who after a
twenty-year absence returns to his town. He muses that poets are
like cicadas. "If the calamities and misfortunes of life permit us,
we sing, we sing without ceasing; then winter comes, that is to say,
old age, and we die forgotten, helpless" (II, 111). *Towns* ends with
the whimsical "Epílogo en 1960" (Epilogue in 1960), in which a
group of men argue about a writer named Azorín. They cannot
remember his real name or what he wrote and end by dismissing
the whole matter as unimportant. Such is posthumous fame.

II   La ruta de Don Quijote *(The Route of Don Quixote)*

In the spring of 1905, the third centenary of the publication of
Part I of *Don Quixote*, *El Imparcial* sent Azorín on a pilgrimage
through La Mancha. Prior to his departure, the paper's editor,
José Ortega Munilla, gave his new reporter a small revolver, "just
in case" (VI, 193). Despite that rather inauspicious beginning, the
journey was completed without mishap. The fifteen articles sent
back to *El Imparcial* constitute *The Route of Don Quixote*. From
autobiographical evidence we know that writing for *El Imparcial*
represented for Azorín the pinnacle of journalistic success (VI,
226), but in the first chapter of *The Route* he creates an image of
himself which is not historically accurate, although it is in keeping
with the effect sought in this work.[9] Identifying with Don Quixote, Azorín describes himself as dissatisfied with the present,
wearied by the monotony of his days. "Perhaps our life, like that
of Don Alonso Quijano, the Good, is an endless combat, without
reward, for ideals that we will not see fulfilled... I love that great

dolorous figure who is our symbol and our model" (II, 248).[10] In this frame of mind, he sets off in search of the authentic Spain of old, traversing the same route Don Quixote traveled. Azorín's antiurbanism surfaces in the second chapter where he describes the inhumanity of a Madrid which is out of touch with reality. Its politicians, bureaucrats, and writers believe that they are "everybody," but an incident at the train station demonstrates that this is not so. During a conversation with a man from La Mancha Azorín mentions that the first stop on his itinerary is Argamasilla de Alba. His new friend informs him that this town is known to "everybody" as Cinco Casas. *"Everybody* is Juan, Ricardo, Pedro, Roque, Alberto, Luis, Antonio, Rafael, Tomás" (II, 251).

In *The Route* Azorín uses archaic forms (*vuesas mercedes* [your graces]), cites phrases from the *Quixote*, imitates the mock-heroic, overblown style which Cervantes ridicules on occasion, and, of course, alludes to episodes and characters of Cervantes's novel. In the first chapter Doña Isabel confesses that she has often been tempted to burn all of Azorín's books and papers, believing that they have a harmful effect on him. Like Don Quixote's housekeeper, Doña Isabel does not understand about transcendental missions.

In *Will* Antonio reflected on the relationship between the Spanish landscape and the Spanish character. Assuming that Argamasilla was the birthplace of Don Quixote, Azorín now explores the question of why this particular village was the cradle of the most illustrious of knights-errant. What was there about it that made Don Quixote what he was? Azorín finds the answer in the past history of the town and in its geographical setting. For information on the history of the village he turns to the topographical reports prepared during the reign of Philip II. Because of epidemics, the town was twice moved from its original site, hence Azorín's description of it as a "town errant" (*un pueblo andante*). These moves, he suggests, created an atmosphere of restlessness and anxiety which was aggravated by floods and plagues of locusts. Equally important is the environmental influence. The town lies in the midst of a vast plain which stretches to infinity beneath an equally boundless sky. Within this setting the spirit soars, untrammeled by mundane realities, impelled by inexplicable longings. Here have been born strong-willed, independent-minded adventurers and solitary, quixotic dreamers.

Azorín returns again and again to the theme of the monotony of the landscape. En route to the cave of Montesinos he writes: "Already the chronicler feels oppressed, overwhelmed, exasperated, enervated, driven to despair, to hallucinations by the continuing, intense, monotonous view of the plains of fallow land, of the plains of unplowed land, of the plains covered with an imperceptible, faint verdure" (II, 288). The length of this sentence, in conjunction with the use of repetition and of words which are similar in meaning, effectively impresses on the reader the sensation of monotony which Azorín wishes to convey. A few lines later he describes another panorama which is "no less oppressing, no less monotonous, no less uniform" (II, 289).

The closing chapter reemphasizes that Don Quixote is a product of La Mancha. "In these lands [of la Mancha] don't you begin to understand the dreams, the delusions, the wild imaginings of the great madman?" (II, 315). Azorín goes on to draw a correlation between Don Quixote and the history of Spain, characterized by moments of "mad, unreasoned, and impetuous fantasy" (II, 317) in which the country suddenly breaks out of its inaction only to fall back into stagnation. He concludes that in *Don Quixote* Cervantes condemned unbridled, vain fantasy but not that love of ideals or those illusions which are indispensable to the fulfillment of all great and generous human undertakings on both the national and the individual level.

Argamasilla's past offers examples of the same lack of sustained effort and alternation between action and inaction which were portrayed in the prologue of *Will*. The history of the town is one of projects not carried through, as evinced by its unfinished church, canals which never passed beyond the planning stage, a railroad that was never built. It is obvious that Argamasilla is as likely to destroy as to strengthen wills. In "Ambiente de Argamasilla" (The Atmosphere of Argamasilla) Azorín contrasts La Mancha with southeastern Spain, and yet he finds in La Mancha what he had already found in Monóvar and Yecla: age-old resignation, immobility, tedium, the problem of how to fill the endless hours which creep by against a background of tolling bells and ticking clocks. This poses a problem: if man is a product of his environment, and La Mancha and the Levant are quite different, how can the effect of those two differing environments be almost identical? The answer appears to be twofold. First, emotion, not logic, guides Azorín. Second, he projects his own state of mind upon the landscape; he "discovers" in it what lies in his own character and "finds" in the external world an expression of his personal preoccupations. As one critic has succinctly put it, "Azorín's Spain is Azorín projected on to people and places."[11]

On his journey Azorín finds that much has changed since the time of Cervantes. Only a few traces remain of the inn of Puerto Lápice, where Don Quixote was knighted. What was once the residence of the peerless Dulcinea, "the most admirable of all Manchegan princesses" (II, 307), is now an oil mill. El Toboso is silent, ruined, a mere shadow of what it once was. But the spirit of Don Quixote has survived, and the various villages of the area stoutly defend their claims to connection with the author or the characters of *Don Quixote*. Don Cándido of Argamasilla is appalled by the invidious suggestion that Don Quixote never lived in that town and assumes that such a prejudicial rumor must have been spread by the jealous residents of a nearby village. Don Silverio insists that Cervantes's grandfather was from El Toboso and that Cervantes was from Alcázar de San Juan, regardless of what Cervantine scholars may assert. Although the residents of Criptana take pride in being Sanchos rather than Quixotes, Azorín detects more than a bit of *quijotismo* in them, too. One of the most quixotic figures is the Doctor Dekker of the article appended to the book as a brief guide for those foreigners who visit Spain on the occasion of the tercentenary. Doctor Dekker, Fellow of the Royal College of Surgeons, has come to Spain to write a book to be titled "The time they lose in Spain" (Azorín's translation).[12] He is a "mad Englishman" who dashes about Madrid with pencil couched (*con el lápiz en ristre*), exclaiming, "The best in the world!" despite the long delays or postponements which meet his every request.

Antonio of *Antonio Azorín* declared that one must do more than just read the classics of Spanish literature. One must live them, contemplate the same landscapes as did Cervantes or Lope de Vega, stay in the same inns, chat with the same types of people— muleteers and hidalgos—and journey across the same dusty plains. This is what Azorín has done in *The Route of Don Quixote*.

III   España *(Spain)*

During his mid-thirties Azorín takes stock of his life to date. The passing of youthful illusions and the gaining of experience have brought about a new attitude. The prologue to *Spain* (1909) declares that he is now less preoccupied by color and form than by the "eternal, hidden rhythm of things" (II, 445). This concern with inner essence rather than external appearance will, he predicts, be a lasting one. He envisions his future as follows: "We will withdraw within ourselves; we will rely on others less than on ourselves; beneath appearances of affability, we will disdain many people; we will look with profound respect upon the mystery of life; we will show understanding toward the mistakes others make; and we will display forbearance and we will resign ourselves, in short, calmly, without spiritual tension, without any tragic stance, to the irremediable" (II, 446). Withdrawal, self-limitation, contemplation, and tolerance: these will be the hallmarks of much of his future work.

This attitude of forbearance is well exemplified by the characters of two of the sketches. "Vida de un labrantín" (The Life of a Poor Farmer) is a tribute to a nameless, hardworking, God-fearing man. He knows nothing about politics, does not think about the future, and has no book learning, but he knows a great deal about the world of nature and accepts all that happens as God's will. The words with which he meets each new misfortune—"What can we do?"—are a manifestation of "his beautiful resignation, his beautiful serenity" (II, 500). Only five years earlier, in *The Confessions of a Little Philosopher*, that same "What can we do?" was cited as one of three phrases which summed up the depression and inertia of the Spaniard, characteristics which were implicitly criticized. Resignation, however, is now "beautiful," as is a sustaining religious faith. The protagonist of "Toscano, o la conformidad" (Toscano, or Forbearance) is a man who has lost everything yet never complains. After all, he has at his disposal the National Library, the Prado museum, and the Retiro park. He is an example of the fact that the key to spiritual peace lies in accepting what cannot be remedied.

Spain, subtitled *Hombres y paisajes* (Men and Landscapes), is a cross between the studies of provincial life contained in *Towns* and the volumes of literary criticism published between 1912 and 1915.[13] A number of the sketches which make up the first half of the volume are comments on books or paintings or are portraits of their creators. Part of the pleasure of reading these pieces derives from Azorín's allowing us to identify the author or work being discussed. He begins "Don José Nieto (1656)" by saying, "You all know Don José Nieto" (II, 467). After allowing us a moment to rack our brains, he describes the painting by Don Diego in which Nieto appears. The surname Velázquez and the title *Las Meninas* are never mentioned, for these details would be superfluous. Azorín then proceeds to spin a brief fantasy as to why Nieto is posed in the doorway in the background of the painting. "Delicado (1530)" is a portrait of an Andalusian village priest—kind, affable, epicurean—who spent his youth in Rome. Azorín saves for the last line the identification of this Delicado as the author of *La lozana andaluza* (The Exuberant Andalusian). In writing about the literature of the past it is often the most minor of characters who awaken Azorín's interest. In Cervantes's *La ilustre fregona* (The Illustrious Kitchen Maid) a girl named Marinilla is mentioned in passing. Azorín wonders what she was like, what she did at the inn where she was employed, and if she was fond of singing.

The way in which he recreates the past, making it live for the reader, can be seen by looking at "Unas sombrereras (1520)" (Some Hat Makers). He begins by introducing five of his friends to another group of friends, his readers. "Do you know Gerarda? And Fenisa? And Isabel? And Raquel? And Guiomar?" (II, 449). The use of first names and a brief description of these girls serves to individualize each of them, and diminutives (*toledanitas, sombrereritas, uñas combaditas, labios coloraditos*) convey familiarity and affection. Another question—"Do not these historic, legendary, noble Spanish industries attract you?" (II, 450)—leads to an enumeration of the goods for which Spain is famous: silks from Murcia, Valencia and Seville, gloves from Ocaña, spurs from Ajofrín, pottery from Talavera, and swords from Toledo. References to historical figures (Isabella the Catholic), painters (Pantoja, Velázquez), and writers (Cervantes, Gracián) who are roughly contemporaneous with the period being recreated help evoke the appropriate atmosphere. The milliners intone traditional ballads. Guiomar has green eyes like her compatriot Melibea. Nearby lives the poor hidalgo of *Lazarillo de Tormes*, "whom we are yet to visit this morning" (II, 451). We (Azorín and his readers), historical figures, authors, and their characters all coexist in a past made present. The use in the sketch of the present and present-progressive tenses and of the demonstrative "this" heightens the impression that we all are actually in Toledo, where we hear the hum of the spinning wheels and the mischievous laughter of the hat makers.

For his sketches Azorín often uses names which are reminiscent of an earlier age as a means of evoking the atmosphere of a city and capturing its essence. In "Una ciudad castellana" (A Castilian City) he mentions streets named Afflictions, Sellers of Wine Bags, Tanneries, Broken Gate, Bread and Charcoal, Old Flour Mills, Lay Brothers, Little Peasant, and Street of the Duennas. The city's three old inns bear the names Souls in Purgatory, Inn of the Moon, Inn of Antón Gallardo. The last of these displays a sign announcing the availability of straw, barley, and water. Water-driven flour mills are still in use, as are ancient presses for the extraction of olive oil. The past is very much part of the present.

"En la montaña" (On the Mountain) is an illustration of how Azorín humanizes the landscape and identifies with it.[14] In this sketch he comments on his love for mountains and the sensation of peace and well-being which they induce. A mountain seen on the horizon, standing out against a limpid sky, is more than just a visual image recorded by the eye. It is "an image engraved upon our soul" (II, 507). Nature is imbued with spirit: shafts of light "bathe" the peaks and "caress" the knolls. The pine trees which dot the slopes are not cultivated for their resin; they are "free and happy." The particular landscape described is one with which personal memories are associated, one which is living and has been lived (engraved upon the soul). From the summit of the mountain Azorín looks down on the places he frequented as a child and adolescent. On the plain below he sees old roads which twist and turn. Along these roads he has borne his sadness, his disappointments. Nature also speaks to Azorín's need for permanence. When his eye lights on the gully of Fernando, he reflects that this gully, named after an unknown individual, will outlive any man-made monument. The tranquility of this idyllic scene, he concludes, is worth more than all the pleasures which cities can offer.

IV   Castilla (Castile)

Many of Azorín's collections of essays are heterogeneous in nature, being made up of pieces which had already been published separately and often over a period of years. Castile (1912), in contrast, is characterized by unity of vision and technique. The four sketches which had appeared in Blanco y Negro and ABC antedated the publication of the book by only a matter of weeks. The prologue explains that Azorín has sought "to imprison a particle of the spirit of Castile" and that "a preoccupation with the power of time constitutes the spiritual background of these sketches" (II, 665). In them he has ignored the superficial and ostentatious events of history, concentrating instead on intrahistoric reality.

The analysis of the structure of *Castile* by Juan Manuel Rozas brings out Azorín's careful ordering of the sketches in four groups.[15] The first consists of four essays—two on railways, one on various types of inns, one on bullfighting—in which Azorín points up the contrast between the traditionalism and resistance to change of Spain and the more progressive spirit of other European countries. In the mid-nineteenth century, for example, many Spaniards opposed the construction of a railroad linking their country with France, preferring to remain isolated. The essay on inns utilizes descriptions by Spanish writers which testify to the noise, wretched furnishings, and lack of comfort or cleanliness with which the traveler has to cope in Spain. These conditions are corroborated by Richard Ford, who in his *Handbook for Travellers in Spain* describes a Segovian inn as one of the worst in the country. As concerns bullfighting, the cruelty displayed in the ring and in the stands is for Azorín an indication of the barbarism of his country.[16] Speaking of an Englishman's account of his journeys to Spain in the early 1800s, Azorín notes that if he had attended a *corrida* it is unlikely that he would have been able to comprehend the public's wild enthusiasm. These four essays present Azorín as very much the *noventayochista*, critical of the backwardness of Spain and desirous of a more civilized attitude on the part of his countrymen.

The second and least cohesive unit of the book includes three poetic meditations on time and space in relation to Castile. In "A City and a Balcony" Azorín portrays a Castilian city in three different eras. In "La catedral" (The Cathedral) he traces the history of an edifice constructed in Roman times as a bathhouse, turned into a palace by a Gothic king and then into a church in the early tenth century, demolished by Almanzor at the end of that same century, rebuilt a few years later, added to and remodeled in succeeding centuries. The brevity of the lives of individual men—Romans, Visigoths, Arabs, Christians—contrasts with the duration of the construction with which they were in some way associated. The cathedral itself, "the same and yet different through the centuries" (II, 700), can be seen as an image of Spain. "El Mar" (The Sea) is constructed around the phrase "Castile cannot see the sea" ("Castilla no puede ver el mar"). Perennially inter-

ested in the relationship between landscape and character, Azorín
notes the differences between melancholy Castile with its sere,
dusty plains, old women in mourning, and sallow-faced peasants,
and Spain's Mediterranean and Atlantic coastlines with their fresh
sea breezes and busy ports. Geographically and mentally Castile is
locked in.

For each of the sketches of the third block Azorín utilizes as his
starting point an earlier literary work, changing or adapting it so
as to explore the effects of the passage of time. "The Clouds," in
which Calixto is seen eighteen years after his first encounter with
Melibea in the *Celestina*, is the only sketch in which Azorín radi-
cally alters the original text. By doing so he illustrates the concept
of eternal recurrence. Describing the garden where Calixto sits
watching the clouds drift by, Azorín mentions the contrast between immutable cypresses and ephemeral roses, a traditional
symbol of the brevity of life. "Lo fatal" (The Inevitable) picks up
the story of the life of the hidalgo of *Lazarillo de Tormes* ten years
after his days in Toledo. He is now back in Valladolid. Because of
an inheritance he is able to live in the style which befits a gentleman, but fortune seems to be toying with him, for as his finances
have prospered his health has declined, and he cannot enjoy his
wealth. The barking of a dog in the night—a premonition of
death—causes him inexpressible anguish. One day he decides to
return to Toledo to visit his former servant Lazarillo, and it is in
that city that a portrait of the long-faced, sunken-eyed hidalgo is
painted. The observation that it is generally believed that the
painter was El Greco is an example of Azorín's interweaving of the
planes of fiction and reality.

"La fragancia del vaso" (The Fragrance of the Glass) provides
an epilogue to one of Cervantes's exemplary novels. The "illustrious kitchen maid" Constanza now leads a humdrum existence
in Burgos. From time to time she recalls with nostalgia the incessant activity and continual surprises of the days when she served in
a Toledan inn. After twenty-five years, she revisits the inn and
finds that no one remembers her. Azorín reminds us that we cannot relive the past. All we can do is preserve the memory of it, that
is to say, the fragrance of the glass from which we have drunk. In
the final sketch of this section, based on *La tía fingida* (The False
Aunt), which Azorín attributes to Cervantes, a student at the
University of Salamanca marries a young woman with a decidedly
shady past. She soon reverts to her old ways, and her husband is

forced to return to a solitary existence. Every afternoon he sits by the river and watches the water flow by as it has done for thousands of years, hears the endless sound of the millclapper, and observes people cross a nearby bridge, as they have done for centuries. Like the poet Ovid, the protagonist wonders what it has profited him to be born. Throughout this section of the book the predominant impression is one of loss: lost youth, lost happiness, lost dreams. The melancholy of the protagonists of the four sketches stems from their awareness of the monotony of existence and the inevitability of dissolution.

The fourth section of *Castile* demonstrates the effect of the passing of time in the lives of nameless characters invented by Azorín. The principal setting for "Una flauta en la noche" (A Flute in the Night) is an old Castilian city where a similar situation is enacted in three moments in time. In 1820 a white-haired man listens as a young boy plays a melody on the flute. In 1870 an elderly man (the boy of paragraph one of the sketch) is accompanied by two boys. One plays a melody on the flute; the other listens entranced and then goes home and pores over his books. The pattern is interrupted in the third paragraph, which is set off within parentheses. In it the second boy of paragraph two is now a mature man living in Madrid. He is an unsuccessful poet and has been alone since the death of his wife and daughter. In 1900 the poet returns to the old Castilian city and lodges in the house where he lived as a child. While wandering through the streets he comes upon an elderly man listening to a boy play the flute. Overcome by a feeling of unbearable sadness, the poet presses his hand to his breast.

As noted in Chapter 1, the concept of eternal recurrence provides for a type of permanence and continuity. In "A Flute in the Night" paragraphs one, two, and four (set in 1820, 1870, and 1900) illustrate continuity on the level of mankind. Each new generation follows in the footsteps of its predecessor and most individuals, as represented by the repeated figures of an old man and a boy, seem oblivious to the passage of time. But for the perceptive individual who either because of his heightened sensibility or his personal situation is acutely aware of evanescence, the idea of eternal recurrence provides little consolation, as demonstrated in the figure of the lonely poet of paragraphs three and four. The fact that Man continues does not extinguish the grief of the man who is tragically conscious of his own mortality. Azorín is attracted to the aesthetic possibilities of the concept of eternal recurrence, but it does not represent for him a solution to the problem of transience.

By comparison with "A Flute in the Night," the time span of "Una lucecita roja" (A Small Red Light) is much briefer. The title refers to the light of a passing train. Whatever the weather or the season, regardless of whether those who contemplate it are joyful or sad, the light shines for a moment in the night and then vanishes. It is "always the same and always different" (II, 732). The point from which the light is visible is a house set on a hilltop. Yellow, white, and crimson roses bloom in the garden and two cypress trees are outlined against the sky across which white clouds pass slowly, as in "The Clouds." The house is seen in three moments, first empty, then inhabited by a family, then empty again following the death of the husband and the departure of his widow and child on the train. In a parenthetical interlude between the second and third moments the members of the family comment on the indefinable attraction of the light. It "is like something inevitable, everlasting" (II, 732).

The final sketch, "La casa cerrada" (The Closed House), is the only one in which dialogue is used extensively, as a blind writer journeys back to the place where he once lived.[17] With the eyes of memory he is able to picture a present reality that he cannot see. The aroma of new-mown hay and the sound of church bells enable him to orient himself as he enters the city. He repeatedly asks his traveling companion to confirm that such and such a detail is unchanged.[18] In the house he abandoned years before, everything is as he left it. A reproduction of *Las Meninas* still hangs in the attic room where he used to write, and a book of Fray Luis de León's poems still lies on the desk. The blind man confesses that he has always been fascinated by the figure of Don José Nieto, distant in time and space and yet very much alive. Azorín is similarly drawn to that which is spatially and temporally remote and yet still living.

With good reason *Castile* is one of Azorín's best-known works. In it he has expressed his enduring preoccupation with Spain and Europe, permanence and impermanence, eternity and temporality, intrahistory and history, reality and fantasy. As Azorín notes in the prologue, he has attempted to communicate to his readers the "spirit" of Castile and the "sensation" of the relentless passage of time. His point of view is lyrical and subjective. One of Azorín's critics has described him as "an exalter of emotion."[19] It is the emotion caused by the passing of time which predominates in *Castile*. Presenting both diachronic and synchronic views, Azorín meditates on the temporal dimensions of human existence. The continuity of mankind is set against the temporality of the individual. Those sketches which have a protagonist portray a person of sensitivity and melancholy. These two qualities are most evident in the gentleman of "A City and a Balcony," the poet of "A Flute in the Night," and the blind writer of "The Closed House," but they are also present in the protagonists of the third group of sketches: Calixto, the hidalgo, Constanza, and the university student.

The major motifs of the book are all related to time: clouds, the sea, the river, the train, the journey—especially the return journey—cypresses and roses in particular, and gardens in general. On the linguistic level the leitmotif of identity and variety is expressed in varying form: the cathedral is "una y varia" (II, 700) through the ages; the clouds, like the sea, are "siempre varias y siempre las mismas" (II, 708); the small red light is "siempre la misma y siempre nueva" (II, 732). The structure of the sketches also corresponds to the obsession with time. With the exception of "The Sea," all are divided into three or four sections separated by asterisks. These divisions facilitate a diachronic treatment of phenomena as they occur through time, as seen in "A City and a Balcony," "A Flute in the Night," and "A Small Red Light." In the first and third of these sketches a similar observation point is employed. The physical elevation of the bell tower of the cathedral and of the house atop a hill permits a broader view in terms of time and space; it represents a literal and figurative rising above the present.

In composing his novels and sketches Azorín relies largely on autobiographical material and his reading.[20] His use of literature as a source of inspiration is evident in *Castile*, a book which is full of literary allusions. As we have noted, the four sketches of section three are continuations of texts composed by other authors. The essays of the first section rely heavily on travel books by Spanish and English writers. Lines from Ovid, Virgil, the *Poem of the Cid*, Garcilaso, Góngora, Fray Luis de León, Guillén de Castro, and Juan Maragall are featured as epigraphs or are incorporated into the text of the sketches. These lines are important as a means of creating mood and illustrating the idea of the essential invariability of human experience. The epigraph for "A Small Red Light" is a line from the *Poem of the Cid* which speaks of Rodrigo Díaz's grief on being exiled from Castile and separated from his family. Over 800 years later similar grief and sense of loss are felt by the widow who departs from the house where her husband has died.

The setting for most of the sketches is an old Castilian city. Frequently Azorín evokes an archetypal setting and uses allusions to features of the landscape or place names to suggest that the locale is Castile. When he mentions a specific city—Toledo, Valladolid, Burgos, Salamanca—he draws on his knowledge of how it has been depicted by other writers and of what events have occurred there. Toledo, for instance, is the birthplace of Garcilaso, the residence of El Greco, the setting of scenes from *Lazarillo de Tormes* and from the works of Cervantes and Galdós. Azorín's image of Spain is drawn from literature and art as much as it is from reality.

V   *Literary Criticism*

Azorín's interest in literary criticism, demonstrated in his first work, continues into the 1960s, but the four collections of essays published between 1912 and 1915 are the most famous.[21] Azorín believes that it is imperative that Spaniards have an appreciation of their cultural heritage, and that appreciation should be based on a living reality. Rather than blindly accepting the supposedly definitive literary judgments sanctioned by tradition, he sets out to determine to what degree those old valuations are still valid. "Everything that does not change is dead" (II, 539), and just as political and social values must be reexamined, so too must literary ones. Azorín's approach to the classics of Spanish literature is innovative, even revolutionary, in the context of his time. He defines a classic author as one in whom we see reflected our modern sensibility, one whose work may be redefined and reinterpreted by each succeeding generation. "We see ourselves in the classics. Therefore, the classics evolve; they evolve as the sensibility of generations changes and evolves" (II, 538). A classic work, such as the *Quixote*, is one which speaks to each new reader; it is dynamic, vital. The classics, insists Azorín, should be judged on the basis of whether they are in accord with our way of seeing and feeling reality; to the extent that they are or are not in accord, to that same extent they are alive or dead. As a corollary to this proposition, "a writer can never be definitively judged" (II, 788). His work is subject to continual reappraisal; new aspects and nuances will be detected in future times. Azorín's own evaluations are admittedly contingent and provisional.

When examining a literary work, Azorín's guide is sensibility, a combination of intellectual perception and emotional responsiveness. His essays consist of his reaction to a particular work, "sensations experienced by a reader" (II, 925), "the impression produced upon a sensibility by a great poet or a great prose writer" (III, 175). The prologue to *Con permiso de los cervantistas* (Begging the Leave of Cervantists, 1948) emphasizes the importance of sensibility as a critical tool. Azorín points out that there are two ways of approaching Cervantes, that of the scholar and that of the artist who aspires to comprehend and thoroughly identify himself with his subject:

> To feel Cervantes is, above all, to bring him up to date. In order to feel Cervantes it is necessary, first and foremost, to strip him of all archeological trappings. The artist is not afraid of historical error; with or without error one arrives at the sensation: the sensation of life—in a certain moment—which Cervantes has experienced and which we wish the reader to experience. (IX, 188)

The artist's approach is the one taken by Azorín in almost all his essays on literary topics. It is important to bear in mind that most of these essays were originally published in the press and thus written for a broad audience. In attempting to popularize the classics Azorín shuns a display of erudition.[22] Instead of a learned study of editions or sources he offers a personal, impressionistic interpretation, "the sensation of life." He concentrates on a detail which, in his opinion, reveals the essence of a work or of a character who catches his imagination. He recreates the situation of the original author, evokes his emotions and feelings, and draws us into his world. The classics thus take on new life and meaning for the present. Azorín's criticism is a labor of love, love for the classics and for Spain. As an interpreter of the classics, he is at his best when commenting on the work of writers with whom he is intellectually, emotionally, or aesthetically in tune. At such times his observations illuminate not only the work under discussion but also Azorín's own writing. In general, the authors to whom he is drawn display at least some intellectual curiosity and critical spirit, intense feeling for nature, attention to the details of everyday life and a perception of the poetic dimensions of reality, sensi-

tivity to the passage of time, or adherence to the stylistic norms of
clarity, conciseness, and precision.

The following brief survey can perhaps convey some idea of
Azorín's predilections and the scope of his essays on Spanish literature. As mentioned earlier, one of the reasons for his interest in the
Middle Ages is his dislike of the late nineteenth century. Medieval
Spain, by contrast, is seen as more authentic, and its literature as
more spontaneous and simple. The medieval authors and works he
discusses are those which are likely to appeal to the sensibility of
the average modern reader: the *Poem of the Cid*, the poets Berceo,
Juan Ruiz, the Marqués de Santillana and Jorge Manrique, the
ballads, and the first important prose stylist, Don Juan Manuel.
He does not study epic poetry apart from the *Poem of the Cid*, the
earliest manifestations of lyric poetry, or didactic and historical
writings.

Azorín has written much more extensively on Renaissance and
Golden Age literature. He is attracted to the sixteenth-century
humanist Juan Luis Vives because of his sensitivity to the eternal
poetry of daily existence, and to the mystics because of their energy and tolerance, their human qualities. Spanish mysticism, for
Azorín, is an example of the true Catholic spirit. His essays on
Santa Teresa de Jesús are all enthusiastic. His admiration for Fray
Luis de Granada was somewhat slower in developing, and he
wrote relatively little on San Juan de la Cruz. Azorín's favorite
sixteenth-century poets are Garcilaso and Fray Luis de León. His
studies on the latter are more perceptive, and he rejects the view
that Fray Luis was a model of serenity. As for the *Celestina*, he is
impressed by the author's psychological mastery and realism. Of
the picaresque novels, only *Lazarillo de Tormes* is of continuing
interest to Azorín, and he writes most often about the poor hidalgo
rather than the eponymous character. Cervantes and *Don Quixote*
are the object of his unfailing enthusiasm.

His initial hostility to much of Golden Age literature is intimately bound up with the belief that many of the woes of present-
day Spain are traceable to the mistaken policies pursued in the
sixteenth and seventeenth centuries. According to Azorín, Spain's
military endeavors in the rest of Europe and her conquest of the
New World led to a glorification of unthinking action and to the
imposition of an intolerant, sterile brand of Catholicism. His early
attacks on Golden Age theater are sweeping, and he at first firmly
denies that it is an admirable expression of the national con-

science. By 1924 he is of a different mind. In 1935 he undertakes a reevaluation of the work of Lope de Vega and, despite some continuing reservations, praises its vitality, dynamism, and variety. He devotes far less attention to the dramatists Ruiz de Alarcón and Tirso de Molina, although he does praise both for their subtle psychological analyses and their contact with reality. Calderón's theater, in contrast, is considered abstract and intellectual. Although he criticizes Quevedo for a lack of profundity and compassion as a satirist, he admires his spirit of protest. Much more to Azorín's liking were the didactic writers Saavedra Fajardo and Gracián, and he contributed to a revival of interest in the latter. He also anticipated the Generation of 1927's esteem for Góngora's poetry.

For Azorín the eighteenth century is a period of transition, and his ambivalence toward it is apparent in *The Castilian Soul*. He particularly admires the critical spirit of Feijóo, Cadalso, and Jovellanos, the satirical narratives of Torres Villarroel and Padre Isla, the theater of Moratín, and the poetry of Meléndez Valdés, the most important of the pre-Romantics. He also calls attention to Mor de Fuentes, a figure who bridges the eighteenth and nineteenth centuries.

Unenthusiastic about the Romantic period in Spanish literature, Azorín writes extensively only of Larra and the Duque de Rivas. His vision of the second half of the nineteenth century is predominantly negative in his early writings on it. He repeatedly attacks Echegaray's theater, a symbol for the *noventayochistas* of the defects of Restoration Spain. His articles on the poets Núñez de Arce and Campoamor reveal considerable vacillation. In *Literary Anarchists* Campoamor is described as unsurpassed by living poets and outshone—possibly—by only one dead one, Espronceda (I, 183); in *Will* he is viewed as a symbol of an era of triviality and vulgarity (I, 847). By contrast, Azorín greatly esteems the poetry of Bécquer and Rosalía de Castro. With regard to the novel, he evolved from initial antagonism, aggravated by the sense of rivalry between old and young writers, to a more benevolent evaluation of Alarcón, Valera, Pereda, and Pardo Bazán. On the whole he admired Galdós's work. In 1895 he described Galdós as a "brilliant, inspired dramatist" (I, 188) and he later acknowledged the *noventayochistas'* debt to the novels of Galdós.[23] On the personal level he was closer to Clarín, who influenced him in his youth. With the exception of the novelists Baroja and Miró, Azorín wrote comparatively little about the members of his own and of succeeding generations. The twentieth-century poets he regards most highly are Antonio Machado, Juan Ramón Jiménez, Pedro Salinas, Jorge Guillén, and Rafael Alberti.[24]

Since Azorín is an extraordinarily perceptive reader, he often provides new insight into the works he interprets. He influenced the way in which literary critics and historians would in the future judge certain authors, and he contributed to an awakening or renewal of interest in Góngora, Gracián, Meléndez Valdés, Larra, Rosalía de Castro, and lesser figures such as Mor de Fuentes. But Azorín's subjective brand of criticism has its limitations. The numerous inconsistencies in his evaluations are in part attributable to the evolution of his literary and political ideas and in part to his "reaction of the moment" approach. In the novel *El escritor* (The Writer) the autobiographical character Antonio Quiroga confesses that for him, and he assumes for others too, books vary according to when they are read and the state of health or mood of the reader. Examples of such variations abound in Azorín's essays. He has often rectified earlier judgments or acknowledged that he has only just come to recognize the merit of a particular author.[25] At times he stresses secondary or marginal characteristics at the expense of more important ones. Also, in concentrating on what appeals to his sensibility he can create a misleading picture of a book. There is far more to *Lazarillo de Tormes*, for example, than the figure of the hidalgo.

VI   From Lecturas españolas *(Spanish Readings)* to Al margen de los clásicos *(Marginal Notes on the Classics)*

A concern with the past history, present reality, and future possibilities of Spain runs through *Lecturas españolas* (Spanish Readings, 1912), *Clásicos y modernos* (Classic and Modern Authors, 1913), and *Los valores literarios* (Literary Values, 1914). In the essays contained in *Spanish Readings*, one of Azorín's more typically *noventayochista* works, the emphasis is on ideological rather than aesthetic values as he presents the reasons which have been advanced for Spain's decadence. He finds in the seventeenth century the beginnings of a preoccupation with this subject which continues into the present. According to Diego de Saavedra Fajardo, the primary causes of decadence are the injurious effect on the Spanish economy of the easy wealth of the New World, debilitating wars, the expulsion of the *moriscos*—symptomatic of the shortsightedness of Spain's rulers—and the Spaniard's aversion to manual labor. The remedy he prescribes is one also applicable to twentieth-century Spain: intelligence and will, greater attention to agriculture, improved education, just government, and a relinquishing of unrealistic ambitions. Baltasar Gracián, Saavedra Fajardo's contemporary, also points to Spain's military ventures as a cause. Besides economic factors, there are psychological and ideological ones. In the eighteenth century José Cadalso laments his countrymen's lack of respect for science and learning, their false pride and propensity for living in the past; in the nineteenth century Larra, to whom Azorín's book is dedicated, points out that because of the Counter-Reformation Spain did not share in the freedom of thought and intellectual renewal associated with the Reformation.

One of the most serious problems, according to Azorín, is the Spaniard's lack of intellectual curiosity. "Spain will not emerge from its age-old stagnation until there are thousands and thousands of men avid to know and to understand" (II, 660). Of the authors studied perhaps José Mor de Fuentes best exemplifies the lively curiosity and thirst for knowledge which Azorín considers essential to regeneration. Through a judicious use of quotations and abstracts from Mor de Fuentes's autobiography, Azorín brings to life for the reader a colorful figure who wrote on a wide variety of subjects and translated Goethe's *The Sorrows of Young Werther* into Spanish.

Azorín also writes of contemporary authors concerned with the problem of Spain. There is a brief essay on Joaquín Costa, one of the immediate forerunners of the Generation of 1898 and an advocate of political and agricultural reform. Paying tribute to Benito Pérez Galdós, Azorín observes that the great nineteenth-century novelist revealed to Spaniards the visible and hidden reality of their country and helped create a national consciousness. Concerning Baroja's 1911 novel, *El árbol de la ciencia* (The Tree of Knowledge), Azorín responds to the frequent charge that Baroja is a careless writer, declaring that his friend's style is clear, precise, and simple, a faithful expression of the way people actually speak. Noting that the nucleus of *The Tree of Knowledge* is the conflict between thought and action, Azorín denies that intelligence is the enemy of life—he had maintained the contrary in *Will*—for it is intelligence that enables us to distinguish between just and unjust actions.[26] Azorín's reading of Baroja's novel is somewhat surprising, for he claims that in it intelligence triumphs, this despite the fact that the protagonist commits suicide, his wife dies, and their child is stillborn. Actually, the aboulic Andrés Hurtado closely resembles the Antonio Azorín of *Will*.

In *Spanish Readings* Azorín distinguishes between love of country and chauvinism (*patriotismo* versus *patriotería*).[27] The 1920 edition contained an added section of portraits of writers he ironically termed "bad" Spaniards. These are men who were not blind defenders of all things Spanish but clear-sighted critics of some of the ills of Spain. In the eyes of the chauvinist, however, the fact that Lope de Vega criticized Spain's despoliation of the New World, Gracián revealed the vices and abuses of his country, and Moratín relished the peace of Bordeaux after the turmoil of the Napoleonic period in Spain means that these are all false Spaniards. As to the French writer Théophile Gautier, an honorary "bad" Spaniard, Azorín finds that in his impressions of Spain he captured something of the essence of the country.

The writers of the Generation of 1898 repeatedly sought to define the Castilian spirit. For Azorín it is a combination of idealism and practicality, as reflected in *Don Quixote*, in Santa Teresa's phrase "God also is found among the kettles," and in the complementary figures of Larra (impulsive, generous, romantic) and Ramón de Mesonero Romanos (bourgeois, practical, sensible). Don Quixote's visit to the home of the Gentleman of the Green Overcoat (Part II, Chapter 18) dramatizes for Azorín the confrontation between two concepts of life. He portrays the impact of Don Quixote's eruption into the methodical, orderly, self-centered world of Don Diego. The latter is unable to decide whether the knight is mad or sane, but Azorín predicts that as a consequence of Don Quixote's visit Don Diego's son will pursue the career of poet rather than a mundane profession. Azorín observes somewhat regretfully that while we are drawn to the idealism of the Don Quixotes of the world we are reluctant to forego the security of the Don Diegos. That comment may have revealed more about himself than he realized.

The preoccupation with the problems of Spain and the search for the national spirit as it has been reflected in the classics continue in *Classic and Modern Authors* and *Literary Values*. Azorín rejects the "official" version of Spanish history and declares that "Spain has never achieved an epoch of true and solid splendor"

(II, 761). During previous centuries money was wasted on foreign conquests rather than expended on the development of a strong economic infrastructure. It is now urgent that the "conquest" of Spain be undertaken. The country needs roads, canals, ports, decent housing, museums, laboratories, and primary, normal, and trade schools. Azorín recapitulates the ideas of Saavedra Fajardo, Gracián, Cadalso, and Larra and in essays on the precursors of Costa further elaborates on the theme of decadence and its remedies. The extent to which this problem weighs on Azorín's mind is apparent in the number of essays he dedicates to it.

The immediate stimulus for many of the studies in *Classic and Modern Authors* is a book which Azorín has just read, such as Agustín Durán's 1828 edition of *morisco* ballads. The essay on Durán's book illustrates how observations on literature are fused with criticism of Spanish history. Azorín begins by noting that most of the *morisco* ballads deal with tourneys and battles, which he, enamored of the quotidian, finds of little interest. From time to time, however, the "monotony" of these scenes is broken by a more placid and intimate vision of a pensive Moorish maiden reclining in a garden or gathering herbs—the type of picture in which Azorín delights. He then visualizes what Granada must have been like in the fifteenth century: filled with weavers, blacksmiths, carpenters, tailors, vendors, and surrounded by fertile, well-tilled plains. All this productivity is abruptly terminated in the early seventeenth century. Azorín turns to a book written in 1612 for eyewitness information on the effects of the 1609 expulsion order. The author, Pedro Aznar Cardura, is unmoved by the suffering of the *moriscos*, for he sees their expulsion as necessary for the "cleansing" of Spain and the greater glory of God. Azorín does not openly criticize or comment on the religious intolerance evident in both the expulsion and Aznar Cardura's account of it, but simply quotes from Aznar Cardura, whose words serve as an effective indictment of the very thing he is attempting to justify. What started out as a book review has evolved into a portrayal of the insensitivity and shortsightedness of Spain during its era of "splendor."

In several of the essays Azorín comments on literary criticism. He notes the lack of good histories of Spanish literature and the need for ones in which the relationship between literary works and the period in which they were written would be made clear. Such histories should include information on how works were viewed by their first readers, for posterity's judgment of the value of a book often differs from the way that same book was first judged. Brilliant success and literary value often do not coincide. During the nineteenth century Rosalía de Castro's poetry was, in the main, unappreciated. *Don Quixote* was neither esteemed nor understood by Cervantes's contemporaries, who saw it as simply an amusing, insubstantial work. Only with time has its true significance been realized.

Azorín uses the *Quixote* as one of his examples of how human sensibility has evolved. The episodes where bystanders roar with laughter on seeing a goatherd beat Don Quixote to a pulp or are amused by Sancho's grief over what he believes to be his master's death no longer provoke laughter, indicating that modern readers are more sensitive than their seventeenth-century counterparts. As sensibility evolves, so too does language. Azorín rejects the narrow concept of linguistic purism according to which a writer must employ only the constructions and vocabulary found in sixteenth- or seventeenth-century works. He points out that today's archaisms were once neologisms and that language has to keep pace with life. The cardinal rule of style is that a writer should seek to be clear, precise, and concise, and hence avoid circumlocutions. Things should be referred to by their proper names, and if necessary a writer should not hesitate to use terms borrowed from popular speech or to exhume lexical items used in the past. If there is both an old and a modern term for the same thing he will have to be guided by his instinct in deciding which to employ. Azorín also notes how the treatment of landscape in Spanish poetry has evolved from the *Poem of the Cid* to Machado's *Campos de Castilla* (Fields of Castile), where the landscape is suffused with the poet's feelings. Machado's spirit breathes in his descriptions of the countryside around Soria. Azorín too sees nature through the prism of his emotions.[28]

Azorín's early appraisals of seventeenth-century theater are generally negative, for he sees the drama as an all-too-faithful representation of the defects of Golden Age Spain, a whirlwind of action, movement, and confusion. His criticism is based on ethical and aesthetic grounds. In *Literary Values* he attacks the idea that the classic theater is a model of virtues and an admirable reflection of the great qualities of the Spanish people. Nothing, he declares, could be further from the truth. The theater, as well as the picaresque novel, abounds with examples of infamy. The conduct of supposedly worthy individuals is characterized by lies, deceit, and all manner of license. Rather than a model of honor, the theater is a school for cruelty, revenge, and false values. It is fundamentally amoral. Furthermore, it is unrealistic. All the plays seem to have been cut from the same pattern; turns of plot are arbitrary and hinge on chance; the characters are without psychological profundity; the language is florid. Azorín buttresses his views by quoting similar judgments by other writers. Goethe and George Meredith criticized the theatricality, rhetoric, stylized movements, and puppetlike figures of the Spanish drama, and even such a fervent traditionalist as the critic Menéndez y Pelayo noted the dubious morality of many plays. There is, of course, an occasional work deserving consideration. One is *La vida es sueño* (Life Is a Dream), but even it is no more than the embryo of a masterpiece, for Calderón did not succeed in fully developing the principal idea of the play, and its secondary plot is "infantile and absurd" (II, 1100). Everyday, ordinary life, according to Azorín, is absent from the classic theater.[29]

The same lack of verisimilitude and logic marks the picaresque novel. Its highly touted realism is, in fact, a caricature, a distortion of reality. Azorín is similarly critical of much of the work of Francisco de Quevedo. According to his view, Quevedo's criticism of Spanish society focuses on the external and peripheral; he flits over the surface of society without getting down to the heart of its problems. All too often he displays a lack of compassion, treating suffering as a subject for jest.[30]

Azorín's intention in his essays on literature is to awaken in his audience a desire to read or reread the books on which he comments. He is particularly sensitive to the charm of the early works of Spanish literature, works which the average reader might tend to avoid in the belief that they must be hopelessly dated and dry as dust. Azorín, in a series of essays devoted to *El conde Lucanor* (Count Lucanor), imagines an aging Don Juan Manuel deciding in 1329 to set down on paper the gist of what he has learned about life. To give his readers an idea of what Don Juan Manuel's book is like, Azorín retells several of the stories, adding his own touches, expanding on the original moral, and showing its applicability in the modern world. Referring to the tale of the crow who is taken in by the flattery of the fox, Azorín observes that writers and artists should not let praise turn their heads, noting that our admirers often extol what we consider most perishable in our work and pass in silence over what we regard as most important.

One of the most revealing of the essays in *Literary Values* is that on Gabriel Alomar. Apropos of the Catalan writer, Azorín states that every true artist finds himself torn between tradition and innovation, aesthetic delight and ethical ideals, his feeling for the past and his hopes for the future. He recognizes that progress toward a more just society will inevitably entail the destruction of many things that he cherishes. This inner conflict, manifest in Azorín, is also reflected in much of post-Civil War Spanish literature. On the one hand, authors call for economic and social progress; on the other hand they deplore the passing of certain traditional values and the commercialization of Spain.

In his profile of the writers of the Generation of 1898 Azorín mentioned their desire to resurrect primitive Spanish poets. This is what he does in the first section of *Al margen de los clásicos* (Marginal Notes on the Classics, 1915). He transports his readers back to medieval times and introduces them to several poets and the environment in which they lived and wrote, picturing the author of the *Poem of the Cid* leading a peaceful life in a Castilian village. There he supervises the cultivation of his land, chats with his neighbors, and from time to time shuts himself up in his chamber and writes of the exploits of a valiant warrior. Since the poet has a special fondness for the roosters which strut about in his patio, he includes in his poem frequent descriptions of their crowing. The treatment accorded the anonymous jongleur and his work reflects Azorín's lack of interest in the heroic. The author of the epic poem has been turned into a village gentleman not unlike the figures described in *Towns*. With respect to the content of the epic, Azorín alludes to the military encounters and then concentrates on what for him is most significant—the poet's attention to reality, as evinced in the descriptions of the crowing of roosters and in the accuracy of geographical details.

Turning to Gonzalo de Berceo, Azorín portrays the monk seated in his cell writing a description of a beautiful meadow filled with flowers and crossed by a rivulet. Azorín does not state that this description is the one found in the introduction to Berceo's *Milagros de Nuestra Señora* (Miracles of Our Lady), but by quoting some of its most famous phrases he enables the reader to make the identification. Now and then Berceo lifts his head and gazes out the window at the real landscape which is a source of inspiration for his allegorical description. Azorín succeeds in conveying a sense of the ingenuousness of the monk and his verse.

Three of the best essays in the book are the ones on the ballad literature of Spain, on Bécquer, and on *Persiles y Sigismunda*. Azorín feels a special predilection for those short ballads which are like an unfinished song and offer a fleeting glimpse of a moment in time, such as the *romances* of Count Arnaldos and of the prisoner. Much of the appeal of these ballads lies in their fragmentary nature and sense of mystery. Azorín wonders who composed them, who listened to them in old Castilian cities in former centuries. He is less than enthusiastic about many nineteenth-century writers, but one notable exception is Bécquer, a poet whose merit was largely unrecognized during his lifetime because of the prevailing taste for grandiloquence. Bécquer, however, did far more than his contemporaries to refine human sensibility. Azorín suggests that the artist who presents us with a new vision of the world and enables us to see, understand, and feel what formerly went unnoticed is the one who truly moves the world forward and advances the cause of justice. Bécquer's is the true Romanticism. In his poetry he has gone beyond visible reality and has sensed the presence of mysterious forces which man cannot understand.

The majority of Azorín's essays on Cervantes's work deal with the *Quixote*, but *Marginal Notes* contains a perceptive study of *Persiles and Sigismunda*. What most impresses Azorín is the prose, which he considers Cervantes's finest, and those characters who are seen only briefly and yet linger on in our spirit, making us wonder about their subsequent fate. The travelers who journey through the seas of the North have been brought together by chance; they know nothing about one another. Azorín regards this book, with its sense of mystery, unanswered questions, apparently insignificant episodes, and brief encounters as a poetic representation of life: a journey toward the unknown.

Marginal Notes places emphasis on aesthetic values and most of the authors studied are poets, but the ideological concern is still present, particularly in the essays on Quevedo's view of Spain and on the nineteenth-century writer José Somoza. Somoza is one of those lesser literary figures to whom Azorín is attracted because of a similarity of interests: a concern with time and eternity, humanitarianism, and a vision of Spain which is based on careful observation of daily life.

CHAPTER 5

New Experiments

A FTER his election to the Royal Spanish Academy in 1924, Azorín did not rest on past achievements. On the contrary, the following years were for him ones of intense experimentation and productivity. Between 1926 and 1931 he wrote seven plays, collaborated with the popular playwright Pedro Muñoz Seca on another, and translated into Spanish works by the French dramatist Simon Gantillon and the Russian Nikolai Evreinov. He also published three novels, a volume of short stories and another of essays. Newspaper articles dating from these years form the bulk of four additional collections. Azorín's intellectual curiosity and receptivity to new ideas are evident in these works.

In his many articles on the theater Azorín described the 1920s as an era of disorientation and transition. Recent advances in the field of science, notably Einstein's theory of relativity and Freud's psychoanalytic doctrines, had challenged previous conceptions about the structure of the universe and the workings of the human mind. World War I had revealed the bankruptcy of the old order, contributing to a decline of faith in reason and precipitating changes in political, social, moral, and aesthetic values. Spain's novel and theater, in particular, were in a state of crisis and in urgent need of revitalization.[1] Azorín urged Spanish dramatists to cast aside worn-out formulae and to experiment with the new ideas which were producing such fruitful results in France and Italy, where playwrights such as Luigi Pirandello and his French followers were exploring the multiplicity of personality and problems of identity, the relativity of truth, and the interplay of illusion and reality.[2]

For Azorín, the most promising of the vanguard movements was Surrealism. In a 1927 article he asserted that it was, in effect, the wave of the future. The old realistic-naturalistic aesthetic had fulfilled its function, and now that external reality had been thoroughly studied, it was time to rise above it and form another reality which would be not only more tenuous and ethereal but also—paradoxically—more solid and enduring (IX, 104). The cinema had already begun to explore the "fantastic, magnificent world" of the subconscious and subjective images, and he maintained that if the theater was to compete, playwrights must do the same.

Azorín designated as Surrealistic the plays and novels he wrote between 1926 and 1931.[3] Various critics have attempted to corroborate that designation, but Azorín never adhered rigidly to the tenets of any group. Instead, he enriched his own art by utilizing elements drawn from a number of sources, and in Surrealism he found certain techniques which he adapted to fit his own end: the further exploration of his basic preoccupations.[4] That Azorín's concept of Surrealism was at best imprecise is apparent in his remark that no one knows or will ever know what Surrealism is (IX, 103). What is important, he affirms, is the "spiritual atmosphere" of the new movement and its liberating influence.

The following description of Surrealism, brief as it is, will serve as a basis for illustrating how Azorín departs from the aesthetic theories of the French Surrealists:

Surrealism aims to transcend the accepted limitation of reality, to bring into literature material hitherto unused, the dream and the automatic association, and to synthesize the experiences of the conscious and unconscious minds. The surrealist permits his work to organize itself nonlogically, so that its pattern may approximate that of the unconscious itself.[5]

Convinced that the intellect alone cannot provide an understanding of life, the Surrealists insist that it is necessary to liberate the mind from the constraints of logic and to go beyond the realm of what is visible and rational. In their revolt against reason they stress the importance of psychic automatism or automatic writing. By excluding conscious mental guidance on the part of the author, they endeavor to reveal what lies beneath the surface of consciousness. For them the writer's role is like that of a medium through whom messages are transmitted. Rather than utilizing free association, however, Azorín does not relinquish conscious control of the flow of images. His is a directed automatism.[6] Also, he does not utilize dream experiences to as great an extent as do the Surrealists, who see dreams as an essential complement to the conscious perceptions experienced during wakefulness and seek to synthesize "the human dream and material reality."[7]

We have seen that Azorín was very much concerned in *Will* and *Antonio Azorín* with an attentive study and meticulous observation of the external world and that descriptions in these two novels tended to be extremely detailed. With *The Confessions* a more careful winnowing of details becomes visible, along with a greater interest in recording the impact made by the world on the sensibility of the artist and his subjective impression of tangible reality. Later, in the prologue to *Spain*, Azorín affirms his preoccupation with the "eternal, hidden rhythm of things." This movement away from material reality intensifies during his most experimental period, and he often alludes to his interest in capturing the essence rather than the appearance of things.[8] In 1927 he declares that the theater of the day "disdains the minute, authentic, prolix copying of reality. It unfolds in an atmosphere of fantasy, dream, unreality" (IV, 925). Azorín's own plays and the short stories he wrote during the late 1920s evince repeated attempts on the part of various characters to escape external reality, and there is a fairly frequent use of fantastic, "unreal" elements such as magic rings, pills, and elixirs. In the novels, however, he does not resort to such devices, and the emphasis is on inner, psychic reality as he attempts to depict the play of sensations and images in the perceiving mind.

I   El caballero inactual *(The Timeless Gentleman)*

El caballero inactual (The Timeless Gentleman), originally entitled *Félix Vargas*, is one of the major works of this period. Shortly before its publication in 1928, Azorín declared that when the book appeared in print people would believe him insane but that the time had come to impart new vigor to the genre of the novel by means of technical innovation.[9] *The Timeless Gentleman* should not have come as a complete surprise to Azorín's readers, since the cinematic and hallucinatory quality of various chapters of *Doña Inés*, the supratemporal perspective glimpsed in Don Pablo's dream, and the description of how he writes prefigure certain aspects of the 1928 work.

When the story begins, Félix Vargas is in Errondo-Aundi, near San Sebastián, writing a book on Benjamin Constant and the women who influenced him: Julie Récamier, Madame de Staël, and Isabelle de Charrière. He is so completely absorbed in his work that he is "living" in late-eighteenth-century France with these four figures. Everything that is not related to his subject has no reality for Félix, and thus Spain has ceased to exist for him. On receiving a letter requesting that he give a series of lectures on Santa Teresa, his initial reaction is to reject the request as absurd, but as the days pass the image of the Spanish saint begins to displace that of Julie Récamier and her companions. The increasing influence of the new image is symbolized by the metamorphosis of the letter regarding the lectures, which multiplies and swells in size until it is everywhere. At first Santa Teresa is merely a translucent, almost invisible shadow which at moments is superimposed on Félix's visions of France. Gradually this shadow becomes more substantial, changing from a "nebula" into a tangible reality, and Félix is able to prepare the lectures.

Azorín's primary concern in writing *The Timeless Gentleman* was to explore the creative process. The action of the novel is limited to a two-month period, but Félix's experiences during this period are illustrative of what is a repeated pattern in his life. For him living is synonymous with creating. Once he has completed a project he must find another in which to immerse himself. "Félix must write, must continue creating, must work without intermission! And, above all, he must live!" (V, 48). Each successive topic provides an indispensable "inner support" without which nothing would have meaning. Life would lack savor, being like a strip of movie film on which no images were recorded. Writing, for Félix, consists of creating a special atmosphere, plunging into it, and then being possessed by it. He feels as if he were inside a tunnel, unable to think about anything other than his current obsession. The entire world is polarized around his work, and his identification with his characters is so complete that he knows all there is to be known about them. Once a project is completed, however, they begin to fade from his mind, and Félix experiences an inner collapse, a sensation of emptiness. Desperately he casts about for a new subject which will permit a return to an intensified form of existence and will enable him to continue living in the timeless, dimensionless world of artistic creation.

The month of September is a turning point, the dividing line between the old and the new intellectual year. In August, Félix is still caught up in the obsession with Constant and his friends, but in early September these images become more and more vague. Félix toys with the idea of the lectures on Santa Teresa and reflects that if he were to write them he would go against traditional norms, trample upon old forms, and discard erudition and archeology, which are the enemies of the living sensation. He would join present and past, portraying a modern saint in an automobile or with a cablegram in her hand, on the deck of a transatlantic liner. Subsequently he visualizes Santa Teresa in downtown Madrid, the center of a storm of controversy, the subject of heated debate in newspapers and psychiatric reports. But in the meantime the image of the saint continues to elude Félix. Increasingly frustrated, he decides to go to Biarritz and abandon himself to stupefying frivolity. The trip is a farewell not just to Spain but to the figures with whom Félix has been "living" for the past months. In Biarritz he encounters an old friend, Andrea, who reminds him of Julie Récamier and, more important, resembles Bernini's sculpture of Santa Teresa. Andrea thus serves as an affective link to the saint. Thinking of his friend makes the image of Santa Teresa appear, and the two images follow each other with such rapidity that they fuse in the poet's mind.

Azorín's choice of Santa Teresa as Félix's new obsession was a masterly one. By exploring the parallels between the mystic and the creative artist, Azorín illustrates the psychological and technical problems which beset Félix. His moments of inspiration and sterility are analogous to the mystic's *plenitud* and *sequedad*. At times Félix writes effortlessly, as if illuminated by a divine fire. Words and phrases flow from his pen, emerging in definitive, perfect form. At other times he is incapable of writing a line. Both mystic and poet attain to regions inaccessible to other mortals, and both face problems of communication. Félix reflects that Santa Teresa had to resign herself to not being understood by her confessors, who did not speak the same language as she. He sees a similarity between her situation and that of great innovative poets whose sensibility differs from that of their readers. Just as Santa Teresa had great difficulty in making her psychological complexities and the essence of the mystical experience comprehensible to her confessors—and to her readers—Félix struggles with the problem of first finding the key to the personality of his characters and then communicating their intrinsic qualities.

Both Santa Teresa and Félix are tortured by moments of self-doubt, and both perceive a special form of reality. On his way to

Biarritz, Félix reproaches himself for not having fully grasped the subtleties of the spirit of Julie Récamier, and yet his very recognition of his failure is consoling, inasmuch as it proves that he has not lost the sensitivity which is vital to him as a writer. Azorín comments that a superficial observer would be likely to dismiss Félix's worries as ridiculous scruples or even madness, but "the images with whom the poet identifies and the spiritual complications these images provoke are Félix's raison d'être" (V, 52). For him this incessant play of the intellect is far more real than the mountains, rivers, and forests of the external world, just as for Santa Teresa her mystical visions are undeniably real. Then, too, the mystic's renunciation of the world is to some extent echoed in Félix's detachment from things.[10]

At one point Félix reflects on the fact that although there were moments when her spirit flagged, Santa Teresa was constantly active, founding convents and writing letters, often not knowing where she was or what day it was. Félix is subject to a comparable confusion. He detects in himself signs of incipient madness and feels that he is standing on the edge of an abyss. In his sensibility there appears to be an "age-old residue of images and perspectives" (V, 44) which he personally has not experienced. Leaning against a tree, he feels the pull of his primeval ancestors and is carried backward in time.[11] In his reveries, images based on present reality mingle with others drawn from past dreams, and on occasion he does not know whether he is in the present or in some past or future world, leading another existence. While writing, Félix pours himself into his work and into the mind of his characters to such an extent that he almost loses his own identity. He experiences various forms of *desdoblamiento*, a splitting or fragmenting of the personality. Frequently he has the sensation of existing simultaneously on two different planes of time, of being in two different places, or of becoming two selves: one is the Félix who is engrossed in his work, the other is the Félix who stands apart and watches him. When he begins writing, he follows a preconceived plan and is in perfect control of his material. Gradually the work takes on a mind of its own and deviates from the original design. Rather than fight to regain control, Félix sets his work free and, once emancipated, it proceeds on its own, sweeping him along with it.

The prologue to *The Timeless Gentleman* consists of a brief dialogue in which Félix and the author discuss the technique of the novel and enumerate some of its features: (1) an apparent lack of system or structure, (2) ellipsis in time, space, and spirit and the elimination of transitions, (3) the creation of images which do not correspond to external reality but express an intrinsic reality (e.g., the letter which grows in size and multiplies), and (4) utilization of the ambivalence of images to reveal the duality of a psychological situation. The extent to which these procedures are actually followed can be seen by examining Chapter 11, which also is an illustration of how Azorín depicts sensorial impressions as they are registered by the mind and of how these impressions in turn stimulate memories.

The opening sentence of the chapter sets the scene: "Biarritz; in the early hours of the afternoon; on the main street; in the midst of a crowd; in the center of a whirlpool; automobiles; sonorous horns; beautiful, sensual women" (V, 54). While Félix is standing absorbed before the show window of a jewelry store, a different scene is superimposed on what is before his eyes. The *colored stones* of the jewelry make him think of the nearby Pyrenees whose stony peaks change color in the setting sun, whose fissures are dotted with the white spume of mountain streams. Another scene is then superimposed on the show window as Félix recollects a landscape from eastern Spain and sees the dry bed of a gully. The sounds and perfumes of the street scene in Biarritz are replaced by different sensations: the aroma of herbs, the buzzing of a bee, the murmuring of a spring whose waters flow over small stones. The colors are those of the reddish earth, the white stone on which the poet—recalling the past—sits, and the blue flowers of the shrubs of rosemary. The chapter serves as a transition between the old and new themes. The worldly elegance of Biarritz recalls that of Félix's former subject (Constant and friends), while the elevation of the Pyrenees and the spiritual atmosphere of the Levant are suggestive of his new subject (Santa Teresa). The allusions to the sounds of the water and bees, frequent symbols in mystic writings, show the unconscious influence on Félix's mind of Santa Teresa and the theme of mysticism.[12]

Azorín creates the illusion of free association, but in reality the chapter is carefully structured, and there is a logical sequence of sensations, memories, and thoughts. Allusions to external sensations, to the sounds and perfumes of the street scene, appear at the beginning and end of the chapter and also precede each of the recollections of the Pyrenees and the Levant. Azorín further guides the reader by using the words *meditación* and *transición* to introduce each of the superimposed scenes. The author reminds Félix in the prologue to the novel that what appears to be without system or structure may reflect a new type of organization, and Félix later acknowledges that his proclamations in favor of the inorganic were an example of braggadocio, for a style based on *disjecta membra* presupposes a firm network of psychological connections. Even though Azorín juxtaposes nominal clauses, eliminating connectives and many verbs, it is easy to follow the train of Félix's thoughts and to see how the colored stones of the jewelry bring to his mind the image of the colored peaks of the Pyrenees which in turn evoke the memory of the Levant.[13] Neither Azorín nor Félix engages in automatic writing. Félix talks about "the subconscious at liberty" (V, 42), but once the first version of his work is finished it will be subjected to an "implacable pruning" which will reduce it by half.

Chapter 11 is but one of many in which the technique of montage is used. Different spatial and temporal zones and different forms of reality are superimposed. In *The Timeless Gentleman* Azorín also makes greater use of scientific terminology than in previous novels, employing words such as *pródromo* (a premonitory symptom of a disease), *catóptrica* (branch of optics dealing with reflected light, especially light reflected from mirrors or other polished bodies), *nebulosa* (nebula), and *bólido* (fireball). Several of the characters are visualized as gasiform masses of different color. Andrea's husband, a dynamic businessman, is a swirling black volume which emits sudden flashes of light and rumbles like a powerful engine. Andrea is a luminous mass which has the radiance of a multicolored dawn and which moves gracefully through the heavens to the accompaniment of soft music.

Distinctive features of the novel are the high frequency of sentences in which the main verb is omitted and the use of infinitives as a means of avoiding a specific tense which would limit time to one plane—past, present, or future.[14] Azorín thus creates an illusion of timelessness or *inactualidad* (nonpresent time). While immersed in the world of artistic creation, in which past, present, and future are fused, Félix is able to exist outside of space and time. In the final chapters of the novel he questions the objective existence of both, declaring that they have no reality apart from our sensations of them. This idea is not new in Azorín's work. Both Yuste and Antonio in *Will* affirmed that "the image is everything" (I, 816, 910)

and that it does not matter if our inner reality does not correspond
to external reality. After all, we have no assurance that what we
term "objective" actually exists, since our perception of it depends
on our senses and they may deceive us. The world is our image of it
or, in Schopenhauerian terms, our representation. Félix, similarly,
wonders if the image is not more real than reality itself.

In *The Timeless Gentleman* the passing of time is frequently
symbolized by trains and train whistles. Félix speaks of the fluidity
of time and reflects that a fleeting moment is as elusive as the
material of a work of art. He expresses a desire to imprison the
present moment, to integrate the world within his psyche. Before
leaving Errondo-Aundi in early October, he uses a camera to try to
capture the essence of all that surrounds him, for even if he returns
another year, nothing will be as it now is. In the last chapter Félix
himself is caught as if in the eye of a camera, poised in the doorway
of his house, one foot raised. The air which fills the doorway is like
the blade of a guillotine which will separate past from present.
Once Félix has stepped over the threshold and departed for Madrid,
the image of the house will begin to disintegrate, as will the image
of Santa Teresa. Once again he will have to search for a new theme
which will provide a basis for continued creation.[15]

The relationships among creativity, the problem of identity, and
Azorín's obsession with time have been illuminated by Leon Livingstone, who sees in Azorín's constant novelistic experimentation a
search for the answer to two basic questions: "Which is the real self
and how can it survive in the constantly elusive flow of time, which
is perhaps only a figment of the human mind?"[16] Azorín believes it
is through creative activity that the artist attains self-awareness,
each act of creation becoming an act of self-creation in which a
sense of identity is forged. Each successive artistic endeavor leads to
a new version or revision of the self, which is constantly changing,
becoming. "Self-creation involves a constant need to discover appropriate new material to maintain the continuity of self-
awareness. Without this incessant replenishment the line of continuity is broken and the heightened consciousness evaporates into
nothingness."[17]

II   El libro de Levante (*The Book of the Levant*)

After depicting the artist's struggle to create and tracing the
development from conception to finished form of Félix's essays on

Santa Teresa, Azorín next focuses on that phase of the creative process in which the idea of a future work begins to take shape in the artist's mind, before the actual writing commences. In *El libro de Levante* (The Book of the Levant), originally titled *Super-realismo* (Surrealism, 1929) and described as a "prenovel," the stated intention is "to give the sensation of the novel in its predefinitive state" (V, 347).[18] We are here dealing with a "gasiform, amorphous" work.

At the outset, "the germ of the future novel" (V, 347) appears in the form of two conflicting images. One, the image of a spacious, thickly carpeted gaming room, is suggestive of worldliness and sensuality; the other, of a simply furnished cell in a monastery, symbolizes renunciation and spirituality.[19] The two images then dissolve into a third, that of a hand about to open a door, but the author is not yet sure to which of the two rooms the door should give access. Various ideas, themes, settings, and characters suggest themselves as possibilities which might be developed in the novel the author intends to write. He considers each carefully, weighing its advantages and disadvantages, accepting, rejecting, reconsidering, starting down paths that lead nowhere, backtracking, and setting off in a new direction. This trial and error process continues for a number of chapters.

The protagonist of the novel is to have a conversation with a stranger who will reveal to him the secrets of life. The author thinks about making the stranger an anchorite from India and setting the conversation in the Vosges Mountains but rejects this idea as theatrical and hackneyed. He is temporarily at a loss as to how to proceed when the dramatic appearance of an angel suggests an alternative beginning. While driving along a highway in Castile there will be a minor accident, and the protagonist and the driver of the other car, an angel, will converse. Another problem then arises. Should the angel disclose his secrets then and there or wait for a more propitious occasion? The author decides to settle that question later and begins to think about angels, ethereal messengers who travel between the empyrean and earth.[20]

Man's belief in and pursuit of angels is used as a metaphorical expression of his longing to transcend time and space. Through the mediation of angels man can "connect with the Infinite" (V, 362), but how is contact with angels established? Is it initiated by the angels or by man? Those who dwell in "the sumptuous palace of Catholic orthodoxy" (V, 357) know that each mortal has his own guardian

angel and that angels appear to chosen mortals, as testified to in the
Bible. Those who live in the orderly house of theosophy keep their
spyglasses, telescopes, and binoculars trained on the heavens, in the
mistaken belief that sheer perseverance on their part will guarantee
their being able to see the angels. Still others are lured into fair booths
by barkers who assure them that angels can be caught with birdlime
and nets. The barkers keep shouting that at any moment a connection is going to be established with the Infinite, with what lies outside
time and space, with the eternal present. This is, however, easier said
than done. In a passage which is reminiscent of Don Pablo's dream
and of Félix Vargas's questioning of the objective reality of space and
time, Azorín acknowledges that time, eternity, space, matter, and
nothingness are merely human ideas, but how can man go beyond
these ideas, how can he conceive the inconceivable unless—like Don
Pablo—he is granted some special form of vision?[21] Although dreams
appear to afford a means of escaping from the prison of time and
space, they too are inefficacious. While dreaming, "from the depths
of the subconscious exceedingly rare flowers ascend to the crystalline
waters of consciousness. We walk through a world in which time and
space assume strange forms. But they are still time and space" (V,
362). It is through the intervention of an angel that the protagonist of
the novel will glimpse what lies beyond space and time. First, however, he must emerge from the limbo of the uncreated.

In Chapter 11 the author decides that it is time for the protagonist to appear. The latter is crying out to be born into the world of
art and life, and his cries are to be picked up by a receiver capable
of registering ultrasonic sounds.[22] Like Azorín, the protagonist is
to be from Monóvar and a product of its environment. Therefore
he will be characterized by delicacy, perseverance, and sobriety.
His sensibility will be a synthesis of the intuition of the Greeks and
the fatalism and disdainful elegance of the Arabs who once dwelt
in Monóvar. He will have been influenced by the qualities displayed by the women of the city—tolerance, diligence, and a
passion for cleanliness—and he will be marked by a painful
awareness of the passage of time.[23] Choosing an appropriate name
for the protagonist is particularly difficult, but after much hesitation the author finally opts for Joaquín Albert.

Once created, the protagonist confronts the author and asserts
his independence. The author thinks that the protagonist is his
creation, but the latter insists that he is a separate being and that it
is the author who is dependent on him rather than vice versa.[24]

The author is inextricably bound to the character whom he will now follow around and desperately strive to resemble. Further displaying his insubordination, the protagonist announces that he has no intention of going along with the author's theme of the opposition between worldly and spiritual elegance, because he aspires to a synthesis and deems the very idea of opposition to be inelegant. Instead, he prefers to bestow a greater transcendence on the novel by having it deal with the problem of time and space. His views will prevail.

Meanwhile, the author returns to the question of where the angel is to make his revelation, deciding that the countryside of Monóvar on a moonlit night will provide the proper air of spirituality and therefore it will be necessary for the protagonist to travel to the city. The description of a train trip across La Mancha toward the Mediterranean and the province of Alicante is followed by a lyrical evocation of Monóvar.[25] Azorín lovingly writes of its history, churches, houses and furnishings, cuisine, and women, seen cleaning, spinning lace, rocking cradles, and kneading bread. He enumerates "enchanting" place names and words from the Valencian dialect spoken in the city. The names of agricultural products roll off his tongue. A chapter is devoted to objects made of esparto grass: mats, baskets, panniers, chair seats, sandals. There is a correlation between the physical and the moral environment of the city, whose spirit of serenity and simple elegance is summed up in a white wall or a pine table. The "Franciscanism" of the Monóvar countryside makes it a fitting locale for the conversation between Joaquín Albert and his angel.

During that conversation Joaquín pleads that he be allowed to glimpse what is beyond space and time, and the angel grants him the power to open the door of a monastery cell and see what happens in the consciousness of a monk. The creaking and groaning of the door as it opens startles the monk, who sinks to his knees in prayer. He then rises and resumes the writing of his book on infallibility. When he reaches the critical point of his work, the colors white and black begin to battle with one another. Anguished, the monk again prays and, as dawn comes, radiant whiteness triumphs. *The Book of the Levant* ends with a description of the beatific expression on the monk's face. The witnessing of this drama is, presumably, as close as Joaquín Albert will come to having his longing for the infinite satisfied.

In the prologue of the novel the author speaks of the mysterious dark waters of the aquarium of the subconscious in which goldfish swim. It is not possible to watch what is moving about inside the aquarium, but from it there issues a transparent stream in whose waters the fish are visible. Azorín thus describes the emergence of images and ideas from the twilight, subsurface world of the subconscious onto the level of consciousness where they are clearly perceived. The author then enunciates a stylistic principle, speaking of the autonomy of words, words which have tired of being imprisoned in the lengthy sentences of an outdated rhetoric. *The Book of the Levant* exhibits an increased utilization of nominal phrases and a corresponding reduction in the number of verbs. Conjugated forms tend to be restricted to subordinate clauses. By juxtaposing *disjecta membra* Azorín heightens the illusion that we are witnessing predefinitive thoughts and the mind's recording of impressions, as seen in the following description of the landscape of La Mancha:

La Mancha, on the outskirts of Madrid. Poplars; a stream. Limpid sky. . . .Eyes which spread over the plain, beneath the blue sky; encounter a green tree; stop; seize that foliage with the glance; as the train races by, leave a shred of glance hanging from the branches.
(La Mancha, a las puertas de Madrid. Alamos; un arroyito. Cielo límpido. . . .La vista que se esparce por la llanada, bajo el cielo azul; tropezar con un árbol verde; detenerse; agarrarse con la mirada a esa fronda; dejar, al paso vertiginoso del tren, un jirón de mirada colgando de las ramas. [V, 397])

Despite the author's proclamations about the autonomy of words, in *The Book of the Levant* there is a logical sequence of ideas. It is true that words are not "imprisoned" in sentences, but they do not follow one another haphazardly nor are they cryptic. The research which preceded the writing of the book is apparent in the many quotations from various saints, books on angels, a geographical dictionary, and guidebooks. The intellectual control which the author exerts over his material is evident in his sifting and weighing of ideas. As in *The Timeless Gentleman*, what may give the impression of being unstructured or incoherent is in reality carefully organized.

III   Pueblo *(The People)*

The opening chapter of *Pueblo* (The People) moves from a su-praterrestrial, cosmic point of view, in which the earth is no larger than the head of a pin, to a close-up of our planet, upon which are magnified the figures of a woman dressed in mourning, a child, and a worker, all symbolic of suffering humanity. The cinematic quality of the chapter, which resembles a scene filmed through a zoom lens, is underlined by a reference to an immense white screen on which images are projected. The analogy with photographic and cinematic techniques can be extended to the entire novel, each chapter being comparable to a single cinematic take in which some aspect of the life of the common people is captured.[26]

Subtitled *Novela de los que trabajan y sufren* (Novel of Those Who Work and Suffer), *Pueblo* is characterized by the same humanitarianism and concern for justice displayed in Azorín's *Don Juan*. The message of the 1930 novel is one of brotherly love and compassion for those unsung, nameless beings who constitute the *pueblo*. An unidentified character who is presumably a writer feels the desire "to return to the basic and primordial; to return to the people" (V, 520) and to identify with their lot. He will abandon the worlds with which he has previously dealt and turn to a study of humble people and things which he now seems to see for the first time.

The first half of the novel consists of a series of views of settings and objects drawn from the world of the *pueblo*: a chair made of pine wood and strawlike esparto, an unpretentious earthenware cup, a shepherd's staff, the baskets carried by old women. (The corresponding chapters bear the titles "Silla," "Taza," "Cayado," "Capacha.") These lowly objects are dignified by the service they have rendered, and their worth is suggested by comparison to precious substances. The chair, bathed in sunlight, glistens as if it were made of gold, and the cup, caught in a sunbeam, shines with "the divine radiance" (V, 529) of charity. Similarly, an anonymous little old woman, with her black dress and yellowed skin, is described as a figure carved out of ebony and ivory. Eighty years old, she is now so fragile that she could be blown away by a puff of wind, and yet during her lifetime she has labored mightily, performing as much work as an enormous electric crane—a comparison that both enhances the magnitude of her labors and implies that in the eyes of the world she is little more than a machine to be utilized.

Azorín does not bitterly denounce the inequities of society; he writes in sorrow rather than in anger. He does, however, make clear the differences between the life of the economically privileged and that of the disadvantaged. In Chapter 11 the elegant leather trunks of those who travel around the world for pleasure are contrasted with the battered metal trunks of those who journey in search of work. Another chapter offers the contrast between the magnificent fur coats of the wealthy and the knitted shawls in which the children of the poor are wrapped.[27]

The second part of the book provides glimpses of the lives of representatives of the *pueblo*: miners who tunnel into the earth like ants; beggars and men who are out of work or ill; pale-faced, undernourished children; and a clown who trudges from fair to fair. A talking miner's lamp impresses upon its comrades the need for solidarity. A dog relates how mistreatment and misfortune have turned him into a partisan of a new social order not based on injustice and tyranny, and a cocky rooster crows that, unlike certain politicians and orators, he is one for plain talk.[28] The next-to-the-last chapter presents two opposing images. The first is that of an immense loom on which the fabric of the people's illusions is constantly being woven, destroyed, and rewoven. The fragility of these illusions, which are never fulfilled, is contrasted to the strength of an indestructible steel net made up of financial institutions and industries. The planet is caught in the grip of this net, and anything that sends a shudder through it, such as a monetary crisis, a scarcity of raw materials, or a war, affects the *pueblo*, shattering their illusions.

In the final chapter the silhouettes of the woman and child reappear on the face of our planet and, in a movement which reverses the direction followed in Chapter 1, are projected throughout the cosmos. The immensity of human suffering corresponds to the immensity of the universe. The epilogue of the novel consists of the narration and explanation of a dream in which the *pueblo* is visualized as a tank of gas which feeds the flame of a blowtorch. The narrator expresses the fear that the flame (intelligence) will consume the contents of the tank (the people's instinct to live) and that Humanity will therefore perish.[29]

Pueblo is an eminently "visual" novel and, as already noted, parallels can be drawn between the literary techniques used by Azorín and those utilized in photography and the cinema. Several chapters begin in darkness and then, as if a spotlight had been turned on, a circle of light appears and an image becomes visible. When the light dims the image fades, being replaced by another when the light is turned up again.[30] Chapter 4, a description of the construction and destruction of a small house, is an example of time-lapse or rapid-motion photography. From the clearing of the ground to the placing of the last roof tile takes some five seconds. The house, which shelters three or four different generations of people, endures another fifty seconds. In a few more it falls into ruins. Man's life span, customarily measured in terms of decades, is here dramatically rendered as being of almost infinitesimal duration. It is equivalent to the cresting and breaking of one wave in the sea of time. The following chapter is an example of a traveling shot. The camera first lingers over the square surface of a sewing table, then travels upward to a window and outward to a patch of sky. The colors of the spools of thread and skeins of silk lying on the table are reproduced in the stars. The contrast between the immensity of the universe and the smallness of man is repeatedly brought out by the juxtaposing of the cosmic and the minute.[31] Another cinematic technique, animation, is used in the descriptions of a carpenter shop, a smithy, and a factory where, by night, tools and machines come to life.

IV   *Theater*

Azorín's experimental plays, like those of his contemporaries Unamuno, Valle-Inclán, and Jacinto Grau, represent a reaction against the realistic tradition which dominated the Spanish stage during the first two decades of the twentieth century. Azorín strove to revitalize the Spanish theater by introducing into it the element of fantasy which he admired in the works of foreign playwrights and by treating subjects which, while not new in the context of his own writing, represented a departure from the established dramatic fare. Despite his interest in the subconscious, however, his plays cannot properly be termed Surrealistic.

Given the fundamental unity of Azorín's work, it is not surprising to find his favorite themes reflected in his plays. His love for traditional Spain and belief in the superiority of spiritual as opposed to material values are expressed in *Old Spain!* (1926). The marriage of the two characters who are spokesmen for progress and tradition represents a reconciliation of contrasting views and the hope that the past will live on, invigorated by an infusion of new strength.

Brandy, mucho brandy (Brandy, Lots of Brandy, 1927) concerns the role of illusion in life, and the conclusion of the play suggests that the actual fulfillment of our desires is perhaps less important than the belief that we are going to be able to fulfill them.

More moving and of deeper significance is *Comedia del arte* (Commedia dell'arte, 1927). Azorín uses as a title the traditional name of the Italian dramatic form, characterized by improvisation from a plot outline and the use of stock characters, and relates it to his own image of the world as a theater in which the same play has been performed since the beginning of time. Performers, costumes, and sets change, but the basic elements of the drama do not, since human psychology is unchanging. The concept of eternal recurrence is also illustrated in *Comedia del arte* through the repetition with variations of a scene in which a young actor begs to be allowed to make his debut with a famous figure of the theater.

The influence of Calderón's *Life Is a Dream* is apparent in *Angelita* (1930).[32] The protagonist of Azorín's play is preoccupied with the idea of time until she awakens to a recognition of the vanity of worldly pleasures. Realizing that inner peace is to be found through renunciation and Christian love, she resolves to make the alleviation of suffering her mission in life. Azorín describes Angelita as a symbol of "eternal human goodness which vanquishes time and space" (V, 450). The interplay of life and art is repeatedly demonstrated in Azorín's theater through the technique of interior duplication, "the symbolic shuffling of the planes of reality and fiction to produce art-within-art."[33] In *Angelita* the playwright Carlos is displeased with the way the actress Pacita Durán performs a scene in which she must pretend she does not know her husband. The scene to be acted by Pacita parallels the "real life" situation of Angelita, who, having given two turns to her magic ring, finds herself married to a stranger, Carlos. When Angelita first sees Carlos and fails to recognize him, he thinks she is playacting, performing Pacita's scene. A further twist to this worlds-within-worlds technique is provided by the fact that the actress Pacita is the female lead in Azorín's earlier play, *Comedia del arte*. In it too he makes extensive use of the device of the play-within-a-play. Most of the characters of *Comedia del arte* are members of a theatrical company and we witness their rehearsing of scenes from several dramas. For one of these actors fiction becomes reality. When Antonio Valdés first plays the lead in Sophocles' *Oedipus at Colonus* he must feign blindness. When he reenacts the role ten years later, he is blind.

The technique of interior duplication is also utilized in *Cervantes, o La casa encantada* (Cervantes, or The Enchanted House, 1931), a play in which multiple levels of reality are interwoven. In the first scene we learn from Postín that his master, the poet Víctor Brenes, is seriously ill and that in his delirium he has imagined that he and Postín have visited an enchanted house and then the house of Cervantes. (Víctor has been working on a poem entitled "La casa encantada" and he has often thought about the travails which Cervantes endured.) It occurs to the journalist Durán that an interesting play could be written about this delirium. The remainder of Azorín's play, with the exception of the epilogue, is a dramatization of Víctor's hallucination. While in the enchanted house he drinks an elixir which is guaranteed to vastly increase his imagination, and subsequently he finds himself in Cervantes's home in Valladolid in the year 1605. The two writers discuss each other's work—Víctor has sent Cervantes a fragment of his unpublished poem—and agree that the fictions created by the artist are more real than reality itself. At the end of the third act all go off to have lunch with one of Cervantes's neighbors, a man who served as the model for Don Quixote and is now striving to live up to the ideals of the character he inspired.

In the epilogue, which takes place after Víctor has recovered from his illness, he and Durán discuss a sketch of the latter's play, which is based on Postín's account of Víctor's delirium as related in the first scene of Act I. Víctor suggests that Durán's play be entitled "Cervantes, o La casa encantada" and recommends that, for the sake of the audience, Durán add an explanation of what he proposed to do, an explanation which Azorín's epilogue provides for *his* audience. Durán demurs, believing that he has made clear the importance of the subconscious, a mysterious, hidden force which governs our every action and which manifests itself in moments of delirium. Although Víctor's delirium has passed, his obsession with the author of the *Quixote* has not, and he is now haunted by visions of Cervantes sitting with his forehead resting on his hand, a pose which Víctor imitates. A doctor assures Víctor's wife that there is no need to be upset, for we all have our visions.

One of the most effective of Azorín's dramatic works is the trilogy *Lo invisible* (The Invisible, 1928). The three one-act plays are preceded by a brief prologue in which a woman confronts the author and asks if he believes that the great mysteries of life should be treated lightly.[34] She also hints at the danger of presenting certain themes on the stage. The author is reluctant to believe that he is talking with La Muerte (Death), and yet there is a disturbing air of familiarity about the woman. When the prompter warns that the audience is getting impatient for the play to begin, Death comments that she too often gives warnings, but many mortals choose to ignore them. Before exiting, La Muerte reminds the author that she is the main character in the human drama. Although she is invisible, an insignificant detail or minor incident is sufficient to reveal her presence, and no one can escape her touch. Azorín, a master of the art of suggestion, manages to evoke the unseen presence of death in the three plays which follow.

The protagonist of the first, *La arañita en el espejo* (The Spider on the Mirror), is Leonor, who is incurably ill. She is impatiently awaiting the arrival of the boat on which her husband, Fernando, is to return from Africa, where he has been fighting. Suspense is built up by means of a series of incidents which portend disaster. A beggar voices the hope that no misfortune will befall Leonor, but she has a premonition that one will. The previous night she has dreamt that she was a cloud, drifting through the skies before dissolving on the horizon; she has just seen a spider on the mirror in her husband's room; and she now has the strange feeling that she is being shrouded in invisible veils. Knowing that she is dying, she misinterprets these signs of impending death as an indication of her own fate. She confesses to her father that her one remaining wish is that she die with Fernando beside her. Before her father can summon the courage to tell her that Fernando has been killed, the whistle of the boat is heard and the curtain falls.

The setting for the second play, *El segador* (The Reaper), is the cottage where María, recently widowed, is visited by a peasant couple, Pedro and Teresa, who are supposedly her good friends. Their conversation about a neighbor's sick child makes María fear for her own baby, and her anguish increases on being told that a reaper is making his way through the district, knocking on doors and causing children to fall ill and die. The motivation of the characters is skillfully developed. Pedro covets María's bit of land, and his wife Teresa, herself childless, is envious of other women's good fortune. Well aware of the effect their words are having on María, they dwell on the idea of death. After they depart, María kneels and prays that her child be spared. The play ends with a pounding on the door of the cottage.

The last play is set in the waiting room of Dr. Death, who holds special office hours from 3:00 to 5:00 P.M., hence the title *Doctor Death, de 3 a 5*. On entering the room, the patient is immediately struck by a pleasant sensation, as if her illness were already cured. Her initial calmness, however, gives way to unease over the ambiguity of remarks made by the doctor's assistant, and she is also unsettled by another patient who points out the significance of the doctor's name and the fact that his office has an entrance but no exit. She is completely unnerved when she takes a second glance at the garden outside and realizes that it is filled with graves. The conflicting emotions she now experiences (terror, rebellion, and finally resignation) are revealed in a dramatic monologue, and as she enters the inner office she utters the words "Infinite" and "Eternity."

Azorín's essays on the theater have as a persistent theme the importance of dialogue, which must imitate spoken rather than written language. He also insists that the dramatist should not limit the inventiveness of actors by spelling out every gesture to be made. In *The Invisible* Azorín adheres to his dramatic theory. Stage directions are minimal and settings are simple. Without resorting to complicated lighting or scenic effects, in each section of the trilogy Azorín successfully creates an appropriately mysterious atmosphere and conveys the anxiety and solitude of the characters as their vague apprehensions are confirmed and they come to realize that death is their antagonist.[35]

CHAPTER 6

A Time for Recapitulation

IN the short stories written during his years in Paris, Azorín frequently dwelt on the past of Spain. After his return to Madrid in 1939, his thoughts turned to his personal past and he published his recollections of his university years *(Valencia,* 1941), the beginnings of his career in the capital *(Madrid,* 1941), his exile during the Spanish Civil War *(París,* 1945), and his life viewed as a whole *(Memorias inmemoriales* [Memories of Time Immemorial], 1946).[1] Not interested in presenting a detailed, chronological account of his life, Azorín's memoirs consist of selective, fragmentary visions of people and places, interspersed with his reflections on aesthetics.

He declares in *Valencia* that in his evocation of the past he has sought to discard what is incidental. He is more intent on capturing the "eternal Valencia," as represented by the fifteenth-century poet Ausias March or the sixteenth-century humanist Juan Luis Vives, than on offering a vivid image of his youthful self. Given the political climate of the early postwar years and Azorín's uncertainty as to whether he would be considered *persona grata* by the Franco regime, his reticence about certain aspects of his life in Valencia is understandable. He notes in passing that he wrote newspaper articles and published some literary pamphlets, but there is no reference to his early sociopolitical preoccupations and, in the chapter devoted to the novelist Vicente Blasco Ibáñez, Azorín does not mention that he contributed to Blasco's radical newspaper, *El Pueblo.*[2] Azorín refers to his Valencian years as "a remote reality, blurred by the mist of time" (VI, 125), and the predominant impression produced by these curiously impersonal memoirs is that of temporal and emotional distance.

Madrid is of much greater interest, both in terms of autobiographical detail and of literary history. The figures of writers, politicians, painters, musicians, and actors come alive as Azorín reminisces about intellectual and cultural life in Spain's capital at the turn of the century. He expands on the portrait of the Generation of 1898 which he had drawn in 1913, discussing the ideological and aesthetic preoccupations of his fellow *noventayochistas*, the importance of landscape in their works, and the melancholy which characterized them as individuals.

In the third volume of memoirs, *París*, Azorín takes his readers on a guided tour of the French capital, describing museums, churches, the Sorbonne, public gardens, marketplaces, and the subway, where he spent several hours each day observing people. He ranges from dissertations on truffles and the construction of the Eiffel Tower to observations on French literature and history. The book is laden with erudite references, as he draws on his reading to substantiate his comments on life in Paris. The city and its cultural tradition, not Azorín, play the leading role in this volume.

While each of the preceding three books is linked to a specific geographic and temporal setting, *Memories of Time Immemorial* is a final recapitulation in which Azorín looks back on the past seventy years and muses on literature in general and the art of the novel in particular, time, reality, and Spain. These enduring preoccupations are also treated in his last novels, published between 1942 and 1944.

I   El escritor *(The Writer)*

Azorín's own life provides a dramatic illustration of the cyclical pattern of human existence. Having begun his career by criticizing his elders in the literary world, in later years Azorín finds himself the target of similar criticism. In an essay published in 1938 he comments on the "eternal problem" (V, 733) of the young and the old. He poignantly describes a "hypothetical" elderly man who does not consider himself separated from the new generation, for he preserves an insatiable curiosity and a youthful spirit. Nevertheless, this man cannot help but wonder whether the young perceive in him anything more than a wrinkled face and a somewhat faltering gait. Of even greater concern to Azorín is the question of whether a decline in physical strength is invariably accompanied by a corresponding diminution of creative ability. Both of these preoccupations are reflected in *El escritor* (The Writer, 1942).

The novel consists of two parts: the *Anales* (Annals) of Antonio Quiroga and Luis Dávila's *Suplemento* (Supplement). Quiroga represents the Generation of 1898, while Dávila belongs to the postwar generation, and in their respective narratives the two writers analyze their attitudes toward one another.[3] Azorín declared that *The Writer* was the work which had cost him most effort and that in it he had exhausted all his technical resources.[4] The novel is indeed complex, and as the reader penetrates ever deeper into its worlds-within-worlds, the boundaries between reality and fiction constantly shift, confirming the truth of Quiroga's observation that "even in the most discerning analyses, the discrimination between reality and fantasy is impossible" (VI, 324).

In the opening pages of *The Writer* the elderly Quiroga wonders whether it is possible for the artist to explain the genesis of his own work. The idea of attempting such an analysis intrigues him and he begins to think about how he would write a novel titled *El escritor*. The model for the central character could be drawn from daily life and then embellished by Quiroga. As the character became more clearly defined, the moment would come when he would speak and move independently of his creator's will. By the end of Chapter 2 of Azorín's novel, Quiroga's character has abandoned the chaos of the uncreated and has taken on a name, Luis Dávila, and by the beginning of Chapter 4 he has become completely autonomous. Quiroga does not yet know what type of writer Dávila will be, but the latter will undoubtedly have his own views on aesthetics. That prediction is borne out by subsequent events, for Dávila carries his autonomy to the point of assailing his creator's works and completing Quiroga's *Annals*. Thus, the novelist Azorín creates the novelist Quiroga who in turn creates the novelist Dávila. Dávila first contrasts with and then comes to resemble Quiroga who in turn is a projection of Azorín.

A further element in this intricate design is the fact that Quiroga and Dávila comment on and quote from the works of other authors, and Quiroga discusses literature with his writer friends.[5] These discussions provide Azorín with the opportunity to set forth his views on the art of writing. His counterpart Quiroga stresses the importance of finding the proper tone and title for a work, of writing without affectation, and of avoiding unusual words, hyperbole, and unnecessary duplication of adjectives. Analyzing the factors which influence a writer, Quiroga calls attention to things, such as those ordinary vases whose purity and simplicity of line are a lesson to the artist.

In the *Annals* Quiroga relates the various stages of his relationship with Dávila. Quiroga is vague as to when and where he first happened upon an example of Dávila's work, but he does recall that his initial impression was that the young man wrote with ease. If Dávila should turn out to be a writer of unmistakable personality and talent, how would Quiroga judge him? Can an elderly author ever fully understand a young one? Behind these two questions lurks Quiroga's—and Azorín's—uncertainty as to how he will be judged and whether he will be understood by the new generation. Quiroga's soul-searching shows great psychological perception. His examination of his reaction to Dávila's novel *La vida señera* (The Solitary Life) is particularly perspicacious. Quiroga, who prides himself on his mastery of the Spanish language, assumes that Dávila has erroneously employed *señera* (solitary) when he actually meant *señoril* (lordly). On discovering that Dávila did in fact use *señera* correctly, Quiroga's feeling of smug superiority gives way to chagrined annoyance, and he scornfully remarks on the pedantry of the young. The fact that color and pictorial effects predominate in Dávila's novel further alienates Quiroga, who is no longer interested in the external world.

Subsequently Quiroga finds himself in a social situation where politeness requires that he speak well of Dávila. That incident helps restore the older writer's sense of his own worth—he is the authority who has "magnanimously" bestowed his stamp of approval on a novice—and makes him feel that he has a personal stake in Dávila's success. Later, when Dávila publishes an attack on the luminaries of the literary world and is particularly scathing with Quiroga, Quiroga is able to summon sufficient equanimity to figuratively shrug his shoulders. After all, he began his career in the same fashion, and no one can annul the value of the works he has published. Eventually the two writers become friends, although they differ in many respects. Dávila has the vigor and assurance of youth; Quiroga has the experience and uncertainty of age. Dávila reads voraciously and can write despite distractions. Quiroga, by contrast, reads sparingly, husbanding his energy, and he requires peace and quiet for his work.

Narrating the *Supplement*, Dávila sets out to elucidate his relationship with and attitude toward Quiroga. In the chapter entitled "Lejos y cerca" (Distant and Near) he declares that he represents the new world of the present while Quiroga embodies the past. It is as if the two men were standing on opposite banks of a river. And yet, in spite of the distance which separates them, Dávila decides that an artist who has created living works of art, as has Quiroga, cannot be dismissed as a relic of a bygone era.[6] As time passes, Dávila comes to view Quiroga as *inactual* (nonpresent), and this vision corresponds to Quiroga's portrayal of himself as a man who has lost track of time.

Their differences notwithstanding, Dávila increasingly resembles Quiroga. The younger writer begins his narrative by noting that he is unconsciously imitating Quiroga's style, by promising to be sincere, as did Quiroga, and by confessing that he is not the same man he once was, echoing a remark made by Quiroga in the opening chapter of the *Annals*. Like Quiroga, Dávila becomes attracted to the ascetic ideal and comes to recognize the importance of meditation, which enables the artist to invest his work with a spiritual dimension.[7] Dávila also undergoes the experience of being violently attacked by a literary novice, and he reacts as did Quiroga. And in the concluding chapter Dávila remarks that his worries about his writing remind him of Quiroga's.

Azorín demonstrates in *The Writer* that age has not destroyed his artistic powers. Quiroga is one of his most skillfully drawn characters, and the scrutiny to which both Quiroga and Dávila submit their thoughts reveals exceptional insight. The novel, drawing as it does on Azorín's self-doubts and fears, exemplifies how the writer takes the raw material of personal experience and elaborates it into a work of art. *El escritor* has been described as "a programmatic summary, a recapitulation, of Azorín's novelistic probing up to this point."[8] In this book, he uses once again the technique of interior duplication and the concept of eternal recurrence, and he comments on such perennial concerns of his as the problems of literary creation, language, the ascetic ideal, and the relationships between reality and fiction and between action and contemplation.

II   El enfermo *(The Sick Man)*

A concern with the problems of literary creation and insecurity about his future as a writer also characterize the introspective protagonist of *El enfermo* (The Sick Man), the sequel or companion piece to *The Writer*. The setting for the 1943 novel is the peaceful town of Petrel, in the valley of Elda, where the elderly Víctor Albert y Mira and his wife, Enriqueta, reside. At present

Víctor's ambition is to write as concisely as possible, using a minimum of words to express a maximum of ideas. He is preoccupied with three fundamental problems. The first is that of achieving the proper balance between the two constituent elements of a work, the abstract and the concrete, the emanations given off by things and things themselves. Like a pharmacist preparing a prescription, Víctor has to find the proper "dosage" of each ingredient. Although in his youth he was intoxicated by the style of Flaubert, in his old age Víctor is inclined to ideal syntheses, but he recognizes that it is not possible to dispense with the concrete. The second problem, that of distance or perspective, is one shared by writer and painter. How do they distribute in space the various components of their composition? At what distance do they position themselves with respect to what they are portraying? How can they expand the horizons of their work? The third problem is that of eliminating all accessory elements and preserving only what is essential.

The desire to condense and simplify extends to Víctor's personal life. Like Antonio Quiroga, Víctor admires the Trappist monks and his existence is similarly austere and orderly. His days follow a regular routine and he is abstemious in matters of diet. His life revolves around the table at which he writes, the mirror in which he verifies his physical identity—his personality constantly changes—and the bed in which he sleeps and dreams. His dreams are so intense that he is unable to distinguish between what he has dreamt and what he has witnessed during waking hours. In fact, Víctor's best writing is the result of his inability to discriminate between reality and fantasy.[9] The steadfast and serene Enriqueta, who is modeled on Azorín's wife, acts as an anchor for her mercurial, impressionable husband.

Time is one of Víctor's obsessions. His personal timepiece does not beat in rhythm with the clocks which regulate others' lives. Every morning at the same hour he pauses for a moment at the same spot in the house. Psychologically the previous day has not yet ended for him, and he hesitates to cross the threshold separating past from present. Standing in a doorway at one end of a dim corridor, he watches the gradual illumination of the doorway at the other end, before advancing along the passageway. During those few seconds of immobility, he exists in a special temporal zone. Now seventy, Víctor frequently meditates on what lies ahead of him. Just as the mountain which dominates the valley of

Elda is being worn away and seemingly indestructible rocks are being reduced to pebbles by the waters of the river, Víctor cannot fail to suffer the effects of the passage of time. His life is now more restricted than it once was, but he derives consolation from the fact that it is more intense. His senses appear to be sharpened, and his heightened sensitivity permits him a greater appreciation of tenuous sensations.

As a writer Víctor disdains the obvious, preferring instead to capture subtleties. In the blazing light of early afternoon, when things stand out too sharply, he feels dazzled and unsure of himself. It is in the subdued light of early morning or evening that he is able to capture the most delicate nuances of his surroundings. He has recently taken to beginning his workday at 2:00 A.M., for in the quiet predawn hours when everything around him is temporarily lifeless, existing in a state of potentiality, he is able to perceive hidden relationships between things. Midday is his low point. By then he has completed his daily stint of writing, and the subconscious elaboration of the next day's work has not yet begun. During the interval, he is tormented by the fear that the cycle of artistic creation will not be renewed. Like Félix Vargas, Víctor's sense of identity is dependent on continued creativity.

As is not uncommon in the elderly, Víctor is obsessed with his health. He complains of a stabbing pain in his side and moments of amnesia. His doctors attribute his symptoms to excessive work and the fact that he has turned night to day, and they recommend that he slow down, but, since he knows he must write, Víctor ignores their advice. Besides, regardless of what his doctors say, he suspects the onset of chronic nephritis and talks of those borderline states when we are no longer well but not yet ill. He has a special horror of falling prey to the ataxia which afflicted one of his grandparents, and he pores over medical books and pharmacopoeias. His hypochondria and fear of incapacitating illness are intimately related to his dread of being unable to continue writing. He fears that his moments of forgetfulness are the prelude to total loss of memory and that his pain will increase to the point where he will have to abandon his writing table and be confined to bed. Even though he is still capable of concentrated mental effort, he may already have entered a twilight area from which he will slip into total darkness and sterility.

The narrator is deliberately vague as to the reality and nature of Víctor's ailment, and the characters offer conflicting testimony.

Víctor tells one of the specialists he consults that he is writing a psychological novel about a man who is sick but seems healthy where his work is concerned. Enriqueta promptly contradicts her husband, maintaining that Víctor is not himself ill nor is he writing about a man who is. Víctor, in turn, insists "with feigned indignation" (VI, 842) that what he has said is indeed true. Whom are we to believe? Has Víctor identified so completely with the protagonist of his novel that he has "contracted" his creation's malady?[10] By withholding answers to these questions, Azorín induces in the reader's mind an uncertainty which is comparable to that experienced by Víctor in the imprecise, borderline zone where he exists, wavering between reality and fantasy, the abstract and the concrete, past and present, sickness and health.

III   Capricho *(Capriccio)*

The opening pages of *Capricho* (Capriccio, 1943) usher us into a hypothetical world which is "neither real nor unreal, but potentially both."[11] In the prologue, "Como gustéis" (As You Like), the author declares that his book is what his readers would have it be. It is or it is not a whim; it is or it is not a novel. He describes it as a literary divertissement in which he has juggled fiction and reality, like a prestidigitator, but he also affirms that there is an underlying seriousness to his playfulness. The overtones of the prologue are both Cervantine and Pirandellian,[12] as are the themes which are developed in the novel itself: the relativity of truth, the interplay of illusion and reality, and the multiplicity of personality. Azorín's belief that life is "complex and contradictory" (VI, 898) and that "the entire Universe is an enigma" (VI, 935) and will always be so finds expression in a novel which is deliberately enigmatic and filled with contradictions.[13]

Capriccio begins with the text of a story written by one of the members of the staff of a newspaper. The tale relates how a wealthy man who is now inclined to asceticism and renunciation of worldly goods takes a million pesetas, drives into the country, and scatters the money about the house of some peasants. Here the narrative breaks off. Its author shows his "fantasy" to the manager of the newspaper, who protests the lack of concrete details. The author explains that he did not describe his character or give his name or speak of his social standing for a very good reason: he wished to avoid all secondary details so that the idea of aspiration

toward spiritual perfection would stand out more clearly. Azorín
thus explains why *his* composition, *Capriccio*, has been stripped of
all unnecessary trappings. The author then proposes a contest in
which others would be invited to provide their own denouement
to the situation he has outlined in his tale. Ostensibly, the problem
referred to in the title of Part I of the novel, "El problema y los
personajes" (The Problem and the Characters), is that of deter-
mining how the recipients of the money will react to their wind-
fall. In reality, the problem is a metaphysical one.

The next ten chapters consist of the presentation of the characters, who are the manager of the paper and nine members of its
staff. Each of these chapters ends with a parenthetical passage in
which the author comments on what he has just written. Although
Azorín clearly stands behind the author, the latter is a separate
being who is simultaneously creator, critic, and a character in his
own work. It soon becomes apparent that the characters do not fit
the stereotype of the hard-boiled, news-hungry journalist. Rather,
all are "infected with the same virus" (VI, 913); they are dreamers
who, like the author, confuse the real and the imagined. The
literary critic lives in the region of the indeterminate, preserving
only a few images of the surrounding world.[14] The poet dwells in
an ethereal realm of his own making. For him "everything is one
and everything is diverse. Everything is past and everything is
future. Actually, only the present exists" (VI, 905). He has the
power to compress Time and everything in the universe into two
or three images. The drama critic, continually disoriented, is unable to distinguish between the equally fictitious realities of the
stage and daily life. On entering a train station in Madrid he
thinks he has perhaps stepped onto a theatrical set, and during his
trip he wonders if he will bump into Segismundo or Hamlet.[15]

Besides drawing attention to the uncertainty experienced by his
characters, the author calls into question their status as characters.
At one point he declares that he is inclined to think that all the
characters of this book, "if they are characters" (VI, 903), are
suffering from delirium. He later remarks that all the characters
of this novel, "if it is a novel" (VI, 915), find themselves adrift in a
sea of confusion.

Subsequently, several of the characters embark on what might
be termed philosophical excursions. The editor-in-chief journeys
to La Mancha in search of reality, but his mission is doomed to
failure because, as the author comments, the region which gave

birth to that exalted idealist Don Quixote can hardly be considered a land of realism. The poet, now identified with the author, travels to Yecla in search of time, only to discover that time does not exist. The literary critic goes to Avila, the atmosphere of that city being conducive to the step he is about to take: a break with the philosopher he once admired, Nietzsche, and the adoption of Santa Teresa as his new spiritual guide. The critic then returns to the Levant, where he seeks corroboration of the fact that he is capable of prolonged and productive effort, as was the generation to which he belongs. The word "returns" suggests that the critic and the poet are one, and the former's comment that his generation has been accused of a lack of will underlines the identification of both characters with the *noventayochista* Azorín. Lastly we are told of the financial editor's stay in Paris, where his tendency to asceticism was strengthened. These five chapters serve as an illustration of Azorín's own philosophical evolution.

In what is the most convoluted chapter of the novel, the manager calls together the other characters, announces that he would like to write "the novel of the indeterminate: a novel without space, time, or characters" (VI, 933), and invites his listeners to be the characters of that novel—assuming that the author of the novel in which they all presently figure has no objection. At the same time, however, the manager observes that as far as he is concerned neither he nor those he is addressing effectively exist. The characters' mission will be to decipher the indecipherable—the mystery of human destiny—and to offer solutions to the problem posed by the unfinished story of Chapter 1. As a parting gift, the manager distributes fragments of the indeterminate and the power to dream. The chapter ends with a parenthetical statement by the author, who feels compelled to point out that the manager is meddling in the author's affairs. His concluding question is one that well might be asked by the readers of *Capriccio*: "Is it possible that in this book all of us are going to go out of our minds?" (VI, 934).

At the beginning of Part II, the author grants his characters complete freedom to proceed in whatever manner they wish, and he bestows upon them the gift of time and space so that they may choose an appropriate geographical and temporal setting for their "solutions."[16] The author's statement that each of the characters possesses his own truth is substantiated by their differing explanations of what happened next in the mysterious house and by their criticism of one another's versions of the truth. These versions range from the poet's musings on the subject of happiness to the drama critic's theatrical tale of cops and robbers and poetic justice. The literary critic, who believes that there is always more than one possible ending to a novel, offers a tentative denouement: prior to the millionaire's arrival, the peasants had already abandoned their house and set off in hope of finding a place where they would be able to make a decent living. Each solution reveals a good deal about the personality of its proponent. The editor-in-chief, for instance, begins by protesting that his fondness for food and drink has been exaggerated by the author, but the character's enthusiasm for the meal he is at present consuming and the after-dinner cognac he is eagerly anticipating is obvious. In fact, his rather incoherent account of what transpired in the mysterious house appears to be the product of a befuddled brain.

Part II is climaxed by a revelation which, if it can be believed, invalidates all the "solutions" and renders highly ironic the use of that word in the title of Part II and seven of its nine chapters. The author is informed that it is time for him to bid farewell to his characters and to confess to them that all their efforts have been futile, for nothing happened: the millionaire changed his mind about leaving the money in the peasants' house. In a concluding passage reminiscent of Calderón's *Life Is a Dream*, the author is told that his characters, his book, and he too will vanish. Everything will have been like a dream, a dream experienced while awake.

The confusion is compounded in the opening chapter of Part III, where the author retorts that the million pesetas *were* left in the country house and are still there, waiting to be claimed. Influenced by his reading of the Greek writer Lucian, the author decides to introduce a new cast composed of famous figures of Spanish literature. None of them show the slightest interest in the money, either because it would not solve their problems, or because they no longer attach any importance to earthly goods, or because they are dedicated to an ideal, as is the case with the hidalgo of *Lazarillo de Tormes*, who treasures his sense of dignity, and Alonso Quijano, who is engrossed with the idea of setting forth on his first sally as Don Quixote. Don Juan Tenorio, we learn, has wearied of playing the role of seducer and of leading a frivolous existence; Tomás Rueda finds life meaningless now that he has recovered from the period of "madness" when he was "wedded to Illusion" (VI, 979); and Segismundo has turned his back on the world, preferring the solitude of a rustic abode to the vain show of a palace. Melibea, distraught over her clandestine love affair with Calixto, has no need of money, nor does Pablos el Buscón, the protagonist of Quevedo's picaresque novel. Now head of a huge company, Pablos seeks respectability, and with a delightful display of glibness he tries to inveigle the author into accepting a position with the firm and lending it his prestige. None of these characters have any doubt about their reality, nor does the author, who alludes to their previous life and describes them as beings who are not the product of imagination. Several of the characters are aware that books have been written about them, and Segismundo has read a distorted account of his life (i.e., *Life Is a Dream*).

The author declares in the concluding chapter that the great mystery of life—the question of whether the reality which surrounds us and of which we are a part actually exists or is merely our representation—is insoluble. As long as the world exists, human beings will waver between the two extremes of being or nonbeing, reality or nonreality. In the face of the "eternally unknowable" (VI, 988) the author asserts that what is real is what we imagine to be so and that there is nothing more *vital* (life-sustaining, essential) than belief.

This position is typical of Azorín's later works, in which the theme of the superior reality of dreams and illusions appears repeatedly. Azorín's prologue to the 1941 edition of *Tomás Rueda* points out that Tomás, like Don Quixote, creates his own reality in order to escape the anguish of being unable to explain the inexplicable. The illusion which sustains Tomás is undeniably real as far as he is concerned; whether or not others perceive its reality is immaterial. In the story "Don Quijote, vencido" (Don Quixote, Vanquished [VI, 756-61]) Azorín writes what amounts to an extra chapter of the *Quixote* and in so doing adds a new dimension to the illusion-reality theme. After his defeat in Barcelona, Don Quixote returns to his native village and calls his friends together to tell them of the marvelous dream he has had. During the span of one brief night he has been a knight-errant. Without ever leaving the village, he has traveled widely, defending the weak and righting wrongs. His friends sadly shake their heads at this new madness. Don Quixote later explains that he is not suffering from hallucinations. What is real is of less worth than what is dreamed, and so he has converted the reality of his knight-errantry into a dream. Thus the happiest days of his life will remain imperishable in his memory. Man lives by his dreams, and they are more fecund than mere reality. In another tale, "El tiempo pasado" (Past Time [V, 976-80]), Sancho affirms that illusion is the highest truth.

IV   La isla sin aurora *(The Island without Dawn)*

La isla sin aurora (The Island without Dawn, 1944) is an allegorical novel in which a dream vision and a fantastic voyage serve as the framework for further exploration of the creative process and the revelation of lessons which man, the voyager, must learn. The protagonists are nameless, generic beings who represent mankind in general and the artist in particular. Their encounters with historical, literary, and mythological figures, as well as their participation in a trial in which a squirrel acts as secretary and a badger as doorman and the defendant's crime is having stolen the dawn, have the reality of myth and fable. Azorín asks of us as readers what Coleridge described as "that willing suspension of disbelief. . .which constitutes poetic faith," and he frequently reminds us that in dreams everything is possible.[17]

The first chapter of *The Island without Dawn* consists of the poet's "reading" of his fantasy about a voyage made by him, the novelist, and the dramatist to an island where there is no dawn, the darkness of night being abruptly followed by full sunlight. The poet finds the consequent lack of mystery unbearable, and he departs on the first passing vessel. The novelist, who at times finds dawn indispensable, leaves on the next ship, and the dramatist remains behind, for the lights of the stage can simulate whatever effects he desires. The following chapter, "Soñaba que soñaba" (He Dreamt That He Was Dreaming), reveals that the poet has "read" from blank sheets of paper, but the idea of the existence of a dawnless island, planted in the characters' minds, germinates and becomes the stimulus for creative action, and they set out to live the poet's dream. Azorín stresses that dreams are the motivating force behind all great undertakings and that the island is real precisely because it has been invented by a poet.

The subject of the differences among the three protagonists and the possibilities of the genres they cultivate is developed in the first third of the novel.[18] Each of the three artists dreams, but reality and illusion figure in their works in varying proportions.

The poet is the dreamer par excellence, and his sphere is the indiscernible and the ineffable. He is interested not in appearances but in what lies hidden beneath them, and in his verses he condenses the pure essence of the world. Highly significant is his reference to Shelley's "To a Skylark," for the poet too is a "blithe Spirit" which sings and soars, "scorner of the ground." At the other end of the spectrum from the airborne poet lies the earthbound dramatist who is tied to the realm of the concrete. A middle ground is that of the novelist who aspires to the symbolism of poetry but cannot totally escape from reality. Dramatist and novelist alike are hampered by the fact that they cannot dispense with plot in their works, and plot has nothing to do with art, which Azorín defines as the capturing and gradation of nuances. Furthermore, plot is always arbitrary, as are the endings of novels and the third acts of plays. Azorín notes that if one detail is varied or one new character introduced, the fragile creations of the novelist and the dramatist collapse. The differences in the work of the three artists are symbolized in the objects which fill their houses. The novelist is surrounded by pieces of pottery which are easily shattered and the dramatist by examples of marquetry which are prone to crack. Far more durable is the exquisite lace which fills the poet's dwelling.

During the voyage which constitutes the second third of the novel, the characters make a series of discoveries about art and life and undergo allegorical tests. While passing through the Bosporus, the poet goes ashore and makes his way to a room where he finds an apple, representing the union of the worlds of the Orient and the Occident, and a silver knife, which is an invitation to sever that union. Absorbed, he gazes at the knife but does not stretch out his hand to grasp it. At another port of call the poet and the novelist purchase magic bells of gold, silver, and bronze which satisfy desires, hopes, or longings for oblivion. The dramatist momentarily yields to temptation and buys an earthenware bell which allows its owner to achieve vengeance, but he figuratively triumphs over his baser instincts by smashing his purchase.

One of the dilemmas of human existence, "to know or not to know," is illustrated in the dramatist's meeting with Oedipus, who explains that his tragedy was caused by his curiosity. Without a spirit of inquiry, however, man would never advance in his knowledge of the world. Conversing with Faust the protagonists learn that man must accept the inevitable and that to try to regain lost youth is absurd. Azorín's belief in the superiority of art is dramatized in the chapter in which the novelist, after much searching, finds the beach depicted in Turner's *The Evening Star*. The painting, he discovers, is more beautiful than the scene which inspired it.

The characters' education is completed in the last third of the novel. On the island they learn to limit themselves and not to squander their strength but instead to exercise self-control. Although self-knowledge, the third stage of the road to wisdom, is attained by none of them, the poet at least recognizes its importance.[19] The island setting affords Azorín the opportunity to contrast the civilized and the natural man. Silvano Arbóreo, a god of the forests, comments on the incomprehensible behavior of the three beings who have invaded his domain. They kill animals for food, read books which make them sad, and think that pills and potions bring health. Their unnatural existence is the height of folly. An opposing view is presented by an elderly faun who is nostalgic for the civilized world of Europe where he once lived and who considers Rousseau's celebration of the natural man to be utter nonsense. Pedro Serrano, a Spanish Robinson Crusoe,[20] expresses disillusionment with mankind as a whole, and his views are partially echoed by a siren who observes that all beings, human or otherwise, constantly defame one another. The final lesson of life is contained in the epilogue. The characters decide that the time has come for the work to end, and they cast about for a suitable denouement. Their sighting of a passing liner appears to hold out the possibility of a return to Europe, but the ship turns out to be named *"Sin retorno"* (Without Return). It is the symbol of the world, in which youth, illusion, and fervor cannot be recaptured.

The narrative techniques used in *The Island without Dawn* are as extraordinary as are the characters' adventures. Azorín utilizes conditional verb forms and a pattern of "yes-and-no," "either-or," "neither-nor" constructions to underline the hypothetical, contradictory, and alternative nature of the events of the novel. In Chapter 13, a transitional chapter in which the potential voyage becomes an actuality, the author begins by speaking of how the characters would sail in a cutter or a brig or a schooner and would put into various ports in the eastern Mediterranean where they would encounter the mysteries of the Levant. The second half of the chapter represents these conditional actions as having already occurred. In Chapter 23 we are told that the brig, if it was not a schooner, a bark, or a lugger, sailed slowly over the sea, although at times it seemed to cut through the heavens. On arriving at the island, the voyagers are greeted by an individual who is bearded and at the same time beardless and by a gentleman wearing a frock coat and a top hat, which several lines later become a scarlet cape and a cocked hat. The author then backtracks, declaring that the disembarkation he has just related was ineffective, reminds us that anything can happen in a dream, and in the next chapter presents an alternate arrival. This time the characters reach the island after a herculean effort which involves rowing through the air and scaling a steep cliff. As in *Capriccio*, in *The Island without Dawn* the characters are autonomous and truth is relative, as demonstrated in the chapters in which the faun, the siren, and a water sprite present conflicting versions of who loves or does not love whom.

V   María Fontán

In *Memories* Azorín speaks of his own art as a compound of mystery and patient observation. He confesses that he is torn between Descartes and Berkeley, between reality and unreality, and that he has long wrestled with the problem of whether to write with precision or imprecision. His solution to the opposition between seemingly irreconcilable elements is the "unreal reality" of his final novels.[21] The characters in *María Fontán* (1944) discuss verisimilitude, observing that life is full of improbable things, which are precisely the most logical, and that in novels designated as realistic, reality is in fact falsified. In short, traditional concepts of what is verisimilar are too limited, and there is no reason why the artist should adhere to them.

The protagonist of *María Fontán* is, in the narrator's words, "a living work of art" (VII, 536). Born Edit Maqueda, she is orphaned at an early age and then cared for by an uncle. One day he shows her an uncut diamond which, when polished, will be one of the most beautiful gems in Europe. If Edit is to realize her potential, she too must be polished, and so her uncle resolves to send her to Paris, where she will be known as Marie Fontan, and to London, where she will go by the name of Mary Fontan. At the end of two years her transformation will be complete; she will have become María Fontán. The adult María is a mixture of diamondlike hardness and softheartedness, sensitivity and thoughtless cruelty, shrewdness and naiveté, sadness and gaiety, love for Spain and predilection for Paris. She is fond of role-playing, often passing herself off as a poor working girl or an ignorant provincial so as to test people's character. Her eccentricities perplex her acquaintances, one of whom is uncertain as to whether she is an illusion or a reality. Her personal life is unconventional. At the request of the aging Duke of Launoy she moves into his palace, her only duties being to dine with him twice weekly and to enliven his residence with her youth and beauty. On his deathbed the duke marries María. She later returns to Madrid, where she falls in love with and weds a poor painter whose prudence and serenity complement her impulsiveness, and the two go off to live in the Bosporus.

Azorín's description of *María Fontán* as a *novela rosa* has disconcerted some of his critics, for this type of sentimental fiction with its rose-colored view of life and its obligatory happy ending is of negligible artistic merit.[22] With a playfulness reminiscent of *Capriccio*, Azorín in *María Fontán* utilizes some of the formulae of the *novela rosa* and, like an alchemist, transmutes base materials into something of worth. His main characters issue from the same mold as the stereotyped figures of the *novela rosa*, for María is the heroine of extraordinary beauty, her first husband is the older man who is worldly-wise, distinguished, and wealthy, and her second husband is the poor but honest artist with whom she will live happily ever after. Azorín, however, has endowed his characters with a sensitivity and psychological complexity which their prototypes lack.

The elegance of the locales of the novel (a ducal palace and the Crillon hotel in Paris, the Ritz hotel in Madrid) is paralleled in the frame within which the novel is set. An introductory statement by the narrator explains that since the Countess of Hortel wished to know the full details of María Fontán's life, he spent several afternoons in the garden of the countess's home, relating María's story to a select audience. If Azorín had been interested in verisimilitude, as traditionally conceived, the narrator's relation would have been interrupted by interludes of conversation in which his listeners would have commented on the story or asked questions. But Azorín makes no such concessions, and it is only in the epilogue that the narrator and his audience exchange a few remarks.

The epilogue is an example of Azorín's spoofing of shopworn narrative conventions. The narrator states, falsely, that he has related María's entire history, and when the countess inquires about the end of all the characters, he avers that it is impossible to furnish such information, for characters continue living their life in reality or in our fantasy. He then proceeds to run through a recital of what became of both major and exceedingly minor figures of his narrative, tying up all the loose ends and assuring us of the good fortune of all concerned.

Irony is also at play in the introduction, for the narrator leads us to believe that he will comply with the countess's request for a detailed account of María's life. During the ensuing narrative, however, precision alternates with extreme vagueness. The first chapter is filled with factual information about the history of Escalona (María's birthplace), its exact geographic location, its altitude, statistics regarding its population, and dates. The narrator is specific about everything except the "indeterminate year" (VII, 491) when the protagonist was born. Similarly, there are important periods of her life about which we are told nothing, such as the years in Paris and London when she undergoes the metamorphosis from Edit Maqueda to María Fontán.

VI   Salvadora de Olbena

Salvadora de Olbena (1944) is a summation of Azorín's ideas regarding the relationship between the artist and reality. It is also one of his most interesting works from the standpoint of technique, because of the use of narrative perspectivism and the way in which the city which serves as the setting for this "romantic novel" is presented. The heroine is the recently widowed Salvadora López de Ledona, who has returned to the old Castilian city of Olbena, where she was born. Now thirty-two, her youth is past and she finds herself at a turning point. The fact that her life is entering a different phase is signified by her adoption of a new name, Salvadora de Olbena. Despite the attentions of her suitors Ricardo Valdecebro and the young poet Paco Ardales, it appears unlikely that Salvadora will choose to remarry. Both she and Valdecebro are described as "ultraromantics" who have reached "the region beyond desires" (VII, 598), and Valdecebro deliberately abstains from satisfying his desires so as to spare himself the emptiness which would follow their fulfillment. Prefatory verses by the Romantic poet Juan Arolas on the theme of melancholy and disillusionment set the mood for the novel.

Since the atmosphere and tradition of Olbena have had a profound influence on Salvadora, it is essential that the spirit of the city be transmitted to the reader, who must be made to feel its remoteness, the sensation of its distance from the rest of the world. A meticulous, street-by-street description along the lines of those found in Azorín's first novels would be completely inappropriate. Instead, Azorín presents four visual-aural impressions of Olbena. As indicated by the titles of Chapters 1, 2, 4, and 5—"Los relojes" (Timepieces), "Las luces" (Lights), "Los ruidos" (Noises), and "La lluvia" (Rain)—each impression is highly selective and focuses on only one motif. In each of these four chapters the city is viewed at the same moment, 2:00 A.M. The rain which is pouring down envelops Olbena, cutting it off from the outside world. Because of the hour, most of the city is bathed in darkness and its outlines are barely discernible. Azorín's description is thus necessarily limited because he has chosen a moment when little can be seen or heard. His eyes are drawn to the few points where some gleam of light is visible, and his ears pick up those sounds which momentarily break the stillness: a train whistle which seems to cut the night in half, the eerie howling of a dog, some hurried footsteps in the street, the scratching of a pen followed by the crumpling of a sheet of paper, the sound of a spoon tinkling against a glass, the ticking of clocks, and the drumming of raindrops against windows. Each chapter focuses briefly upon from six to twelve points in the city. These points, seemingly selected at random and of little significance, actually constitute a highly representative cross section of Olbena: church, town hall, post office, railway station, hotel, casino, drugstore, Salvadora's mansion, a peasant's cottage, and a sickroom. Each of the important characters is introduced. By the end of Chapter 5 the reader has been shown the various components which make up the whole city.[23]

Salvadora de Olbena reaffirms the superior truth of fiction. In Chapter 3 the author announces that up to this point he has been a historian, but from now on he will be a novelist, for the novel is the domain of the "true truth" (VII, 574). He warns the reader not to be surprised by certain peculiarities of language and action which he will encounter in the pages that lie ahead, explaining that the artist's view of what is "natural" is quite different from the historian's. The former uses reality as a point of departure. At one point in the novel Salvadora and her two would-be suitors visit the laboratory of the inventor Damián Ontiveros. Ontiveros notes the similarity between the scientist and the writer, both of whom pursue hypotheses. "The literary artist leaps from reality, as from a trampoline, into the realm of the ideal" (VII, 621). Whether his "leap" turns out well or badly will depend on the reality (the hypothesis) which supports him, and that support is indispensable.[24] Reality is, however, nothing but the foundation for the artist's ideal reconstruction of the real world.

As in *Capriccio*, in *Salvadora de Olbena* Azorín utilizes narrative perspectivism to demonstrate the limited nature of human intelligence and the relativity of all knowledge. The fact that man cannot decipher the enigma of the universe is symbolized by the author's inability to determine the reasons for the supposed falling-out between Salvadora and her relative Don Juan Pimentel. From Chapters 30 to 34, five characters give irreconcilable versions "De la historia" (Of the History), as these chapters are ironically entitled.[25] The fifth speaker, Dr. Bretaño, recalls several lines from the musical comedy *Marina*. The original text has apparently been corrupted because the lines, as usually quoted, contain a non sequitur. Bretaño draws a parallel between the problem of the interpretation and correction of the text in question and that of ascertaining what happened between Salvadora and Pimentel. Both problems appear to be insoluble, for "life is complex and changing; history cannot capture life" (VII, 666). Moreover, the past is modified by the present; history is continually rewritten. Since everything is contingent and variable, Bretaño recommends impartiality as the only sensible stance. The author now intervenes and discusses additional variants of the lines from *Marina*, acknowledging that the textual problem, difficult as it is, is simple in comparison with the Salvadora-Pimentel problem. Both are dwarfed by the magnitude of the larger issue of the validity of all purported knowledge. Recognizing the limitations of the intellect, Azorín's attitude is one of skepticism with regard to the possibility of absolute knowledge.[26]

Man, he concludes, is condemned to partial vision, limited to his own particular viewpoint. Amid "universal uncertainty" (VII, 606), the most he can achieve is the knowledge that he knows nothing. In *Memories* Azorín defines the true man of the world, the man of aristocratic spirit, as one who knows that truth lies beyond his grasp, that it is contingent. As a result, his attitude toward the world is one of detachment; "he is at the same time in the world and outside of it" (VIII, 575). Having seen everything,

read everything, and felt everything, he can look on human folly
with understanding and forgiveness. This type of man, affirms
Azorín, does not belong to any one century; he is characterized by
his *inactualidad* or timelessness.

CHAPTER 7

Conclusion

A ZORÍN accurately described himself in the preface to the first
volume of his *Complete Works* as a writer who had devoted
his life to literature (I, 3). At age seventy-three he felt far removed
from the angry youth who had begun his career in the 1890s as a
political radical and an outspoken, impassioned critic of existing
institutions. That sociopolitical radicalism was comparatively
shortlived, but Azorín's spirit of independence and nonconformity
continued to manifest itself in other areas. It was in the literary,
not the political, field that he was to become a revolutionary
figure, constantly innovative and receptive to new ideas.

Azorín reacted against the style of much of nineteenth-century
literature and advocated the use of short, simple sentences in lieu
of lengthy, syntactically complex ones. He repeatedly emphasized
the importance of simplicity, clarity, and precision and sought to
enrich the Spanish language and make it a more expressive, supple
tool. The vocabulary of the *pueblo*, he found, preserved a multitude of words which had vanished from learned, citified speech,
and he used these words, as well as neologisms, when appropriate.
Richness and variety of vocabulary were essential to the attain-
ment of his goal of expressing the most subtle nuances of things
and evoking sensations and indefinable emotions, despite the inadequacies of language.

The writers of the Generation of 1898 offered a new vision of
Spain, focusing on its intrahistoric reality. Azorín was especially
responsive to the "beauties of the commonplace" and the significance of *los menudos hechos* of everyday life. He was also sensitive
to the interrelationship of landscape, people, history, literature,
and art, and his portrayal of Castile, the "soul" of Spain, reveals
the intimate harmony of these elements. For him the past is a
living part of the present, and in his studies of the classics he
demonstrates the vitality of the literature of former ages, a cul-

tural legacy which he wishes his readers to appreciate. His approach is that of the artist who identifies with his subjects and offers an impressionistic, subjective interpretation of them, guided by his sensibility. The protagonist of *Diary of a Sick Man* asked, "Where is life: in books or in the street?" As the years pass, it becomes increasingly apparent that for Azorín the answer is, "In books." Reading is for him both a way of life and a way of experiencing life vicariously. It is a basic part of the creative process. Azorín's writing is often rewriting: recreating others' characters, elaborating on others' themes, and reworking his own favorite themes. His reading of the classics and of Spanish history profoundly influences his vision of Spain.

It is only in recent years that Azorín's importance as a novelist has begun to be recognized, and there is still a tendency on the part of a number of critics to regard his novels with a certain disdain. Implicit in much of their criticism is the notion that a work which does not adhere to traditional narrative formulae is undeserving of the term "novel." Azorín, however, deliberately rejected the nineteenth-century canon. For him the novel is not a closed but an open form in which discussions of intellectual and aesthetic questions play an important role. As a matter of fact, theorizing about the novel, reflections on the problems of literary creation, and views of the artist at work—often seen conceiving or elaborating the very composition we are reading—are fundamental components of his narratives. Livingstone points out that "what Azorín creates—in his pursuit of novelistic form from the chronological, autobiographical realism of *La Voluntad* to the esthetic allegory of *La isla sin aurora* and the unreal reality of *María Fontán* and *Salvadora de Olbena*—is the self-conscious novel, simultaneously novel-within-the-novel and anti-novel."[1] The unorthodox nature of these narratives, although disconcerting to many readers, exemplifies the dissatisfaction with conventional novelistic procedures and the experimentation with new techniques which characterize much of twentieth-century fiction.[2]

Azorín's art is one of deliberate limitation. "To limit oneself is to concentrate one's strength; it is to acquire a profundity, an intensity, a synthesizing force which formerly we did not possess" (VII, 41). His novels, sketches, essays, short stories, and plays revolve around a reduced number of abiding concerns which form the core of continuity of his distinctive literary world. Ignacio Zuloaga's 1941 portrait of Azorín captures much of the spirit of the man and his work. In the foreground of the painting is a pensive Azorín, seated at a table covered with books, one of which is the novel *Doña Inés*, and the pages of a manuscript. He holds in his right hand a copy of *Pensando en España* (Thinking about Spain). The background against which the solitary figure is silhouetted is the Castilian landscape, with the ruins of an old castle visible in the distance atop a small rise. In this setting the writer meditates on the past and the present, on the temporal and the eternal, on his art, and on reality and illusion.

Notes and References

Chapter One

1. Azorín, *Obras completas*, ed. Angel Cruz Rueda, 2nd ed., 9 vols. (Madrid: Aguilar, 1959-1963), III, 289. Subsequent references to the *Obras completas* will be given in the text by volume and page number.
2. See André Maurois, *Aspects of Biography*, trans. S.C. Roberts (Cambridge: Cambridge Univ. Press, 1929), pp. 133-45.
3. See IX, 1136-43, and II, 900-18.
4. Azorín attributes special importance to the influence of Nietzsche, Théophile Gautier, and Verlaine. Regarding Nietzsche's influence, see Gonzalo Sobejano, *Nietzsche en España* (Madrid: Gredos, 1967), pp. 133-38, 395-419, 480-85. Particularly significant for Azorín were the emotional implications of the concept of eternal recurrence and Nietzsche's ideas on the transmutation of moral values.
5. See Chapter V, "Amor amargo," of Pedro Laín Entralgo's *La generación del noventa y ocho*, 3rd ed. (Madrid: Espasa-Calpe, 1956), pp. 88-145.
6. Laín Entralgo, pp. 19, 200-203.
7. For a comparison of these three versions of the coffin incident, see José María Valverde, *Azorín* (Barcelona: Planeta, 1971), pp. 153-56. In *Madrid* Azorín again recalls the Toledo visit (VI, 242-44).
8. The text of the speech is incorporated in *Will* (I, 953-55).
9. For a list of these publications, see Fernando Sáinz de Bujanda, *Clausura de un centenario: Guía bibliográfica de Azorín* (Madrid: Revista de Occidente, 1974), pp. 253-55. Regarding Azorín's early journalistic endeavors, see E. Inman Fox, "Una bibliografía anotada del periodismo de José Martínez Ruiz (Azorín): 1894-1904," *Revista de Literatura* 28 (1965): 231-44.
10. Leon Livingstone describes the process as follows: "The 'real' author projects himself fictionally into his character and then is superseded by him. Art first imitates reality and then absorbs it" ("Self-creation and Alienation in the Novels of Azorín," *Journal of Spanish Studies: Twentieth Century* 1 [1973]: 31).
11. Various theories have been advanced for the choice of this name—

that it was an attempt to emulate the brevity of Leopoldo Alas's pseudonym, Clarín, or Larra's Fígaro, that Azorín had in mind the penetrating vision and soaring flight of the goshawk *(azor)* or that he was alluding to his timidity *(azorarse* means "to be abashed"). See Anna Krause, *Azorín, the Little Philosopher: Inquiry into the Birth of a Literary Personality,* Univ. of California Publications in Modern Philology, vol. 28, no. 4 (Berkeley: Univ. of California Press, 1948), pp. 193-95, and César Barja, "Azorín," in *Libros y autores contemporáneos* (New York: G.E. Stechert & Co., 1935), p. 265.

12. Quoted in Valverde, p. 283.

13. Krause suggests that Azorín's admiration for public figures like Maura was due to the fact that he saw in the statesman the exemplary man of action (pp. 265-66).

14. For a detailed account of Azorín's journalistic activity during these years, see Valverde, pp. 357-90.

15. In "La vida de un español" (IX, 1441-45), Azorín describes the pattern of his daily life, as of 1941.

16. Most of the books which appeared after 1944 are collections of previously published articles and short stories, although in some instances new material is incorporated.

17. See VI, 185, and VIII, 342, where he cites his conviction that everything is present as justification for his nonchronological presentation of images. The techniques he uses to create the illusion of timelessness in his 1928-1930 novels will be discussed in Chapter 5.

18. One of the distinctive features of Azorín's style is his use of the present perfect in preference to the preterite. This last tense views an event as wholly past, a completed unit in time. The present perfect also indicates past actions, but actions which have just taken place or whose effects extend into the present. By using the present perfect, the past is seen in relation with the present, falling within the realm of an expanded present. In the 1928-1930 novels Azorín also resorts to the use of verbless sentences and the infinitive, a timeless verb form. In the last novels the conditional is frequently employed, because much of the action is hypothetical. On Azorín's style, see Heinrich Denner, *Das Stilproblem bei Azorín* (Zurich: Rascher & Cie., 1931); Elizabeth Espadas, "Azorín's Prose Style: Theory and Practice," *Hispanófila,* no. 59 (1977): 49-73; and Leon Livingstone, *Tema y forma en las novelas de Azorín* (Madrid: Gredos, 1970), pp. 169-221.

19. José Ortega y Gasset describes Azorín's art as an attempt to save the world from destruction by aesthetically petrifying it ("Azorín o primores de lo vulgar," in *Obras completas,* II [Madrid: Revista de Occidente, 1946], 170).

20. When he resorts to a different pattern, as in *Doña Inés,* it is for a specific purpose.

21. Laín Entralgo notes (p. 156) that Azorín's distinction between

menudos and *grandes hechos* is comparable to Unamuno's distinction between *hechos permanentes* (permanent occurrences which constitute "intrahistory") and *sucesos fugaces* (fleeting events which constitute history). Laín Entralgo also points to a similarity in the way both writers view the present. Unamuno sees it as composed of two strata: the superficial one of the historic present, and the underlying one of the intrahistoric present which is the result of the sedimentation and eternization of all the historic presents which have already passed. Azorín sees each moment as made up of two components: that which is superficial and rigorously singular, and that which is profound and generically human—and hence repeatable through recreative evocation (pp. 152-53, 161).

22. This is the phrase Ortega used to characterize the art of Azorín. See note 19.

23. There is a further parallelism in the internal structure of each of these three sections. Each consists of three parts, the first of which describes the city and a group of travelers approaching it; the second—placed in parentheses—provides the information necessary to identify the particular moment in time; the third focuses on the figure on the balcony. The lesser importance of *los grandes hechos* of history (the discovery of America, the French Revolution, modern advances in transportation and science) is underlined by their placement within parentheses. On the subject of time in Azorín's works, also see Carlos Clavería, "Sobre el tema del tiempo en Azorín," in *Cinco estudios de literatura española moderna* (Salamanca: Consejo Superior de Investigaciones Científicas, 1945), pp. 49-67; Manuel Granell, *Estética de Azorín* (Madrid: Biblioteca Nueva, 1949), pp. 149-71; Livingstone, *Tema y forma*, pp. 115-43; and José Antonio Maravall, "Azorín. Idea y sentido de la microhistoria," *Cuadernos Hispanoamericanos*, nos. 226–27 (October-November 1968): 28–77.

Chapter Two

1. In 1897 Clarín praised one of Azorín's articles and gave the fledgling writer some sound advice: "May God preserve you from seeking originality, which if it is to be real must be spontaneous; and even more [may He preserve you] from seeking it in disrespect and in the affectation of arbitrarily swimming against the current" (I, 256). For a detailed account of the Azorín-Clarín relationship, see Valverde, pp. 41–54.

2. On Azorín's anarchism, see Carlos Blanco Aguinaga, *Juventud del 98* (Madrid: Siglo Veintiuno de España, 1970), pp. 115-64, and E. Inman Fox, "José Martínez Ruiz (Sobre el anarquismo del futuro Azorín)," *Revista de Occidente*, no. 35 (February 1966): 157–74.

3. Quoted in Valverde, p. 105.

4. The first part of *The Castilian Soul* had appeared separately the same year (1900) under the title *Los hidalgos*.

5. José María Martínez Cachero, *Las novelas de Azorín* (Madrid: Insula, 1960), p. 71, n. 18.

6. The protagonist wonders if he is mad, as days of extreme excitation and frenzied creativity when his pen races across the page alternate with others when he falls into a complete stupor and is incapable of writing a line. The subject of the artist's alternating periods of inspiration and sterility is more fully developed in *Doña Inés* and *El caballero inactual*.

7. The protagonist's eventual suicide is also suggested by the attraction of death which he feels in Toledo. While walking through the city's streets he sees a man carrying a small white coffin and is drawn to follow him.

8. Leon Livingstone, "The 'Esthetic of Repose' in Azorín's *Diario de un enfermo*," *Symposium* 20 (1966): 242–43.

9. Ibid., p. 245.

Chapter Three

1. During the major portion of the novel the character is referred to by his last name, but I shall refer to him as "Antonio," reserving "Azorín" for the author.

2. Pilar de Madariaga, "Las novelas de Azorín: Estudio de sus temas y de su técnica," Diss. Middlebury College 1949, p. 129.

3. For an explication of the prologue, see Andrés Amorós, "El prólogo de *La voluntad* (Lectura)," *Cuadernos Hispanoamericanos*, nos. 226–27 (October-November 1968): 339–54.

4. See R.W. Fiddian, "Cyclical Time and the Structure of Azorín's *La voluntad*," *Forum for Modern Language Studies* 12 (1976): 163–75.

5. Sergio Beser, "Notas sobre la estructura de *La voluntad*," *Boletín de la Sociedad Castellonense de Cultura* 36 (July-September 1960): 173. Puche's conversation is filled with quotations from the Bible, Yuste's with ideas gleaned from Schopenhauer, Nietzsche, Kant, and Jean Marie Guyau.

6. Beser, p. 171. Other historical figures appear in the novel. Antonio visits the politician Pi y Margall and talks with Father Lasalde, rector of the Piarist school in Yecla which Azorín had attended. Various models have been suggested for the character Yuste, including Azorín's great-grandfather and Pi y Margall (Valverde, p. 195). It is more likely that Yuste is the embodiment of the concept of the philosopher-educator and as such is not modeled on any one person. See Chapter II, "The Philosopher as Educator," of Krause's study, pp. 180–206.

7. Quoted in Valverde, p. 184.

8. On *Will*, also see E. Inman Fox's introduction to *La voluntad*, 2nd ed. (Madrid: Castalia, 1973), pp. 27–46.

9. The character Verdú is a portrait of Azorín's uncle Miguel Amat y Maestre. Amat hoped that his nephew would some day write his biography, and the autobiographical material and letters which he sent to

Azorín served as the basis for the letters which Antonio receives in the novel. See José Rico Verdú, *Un Azorín desconocido: Estudio psicológico de su obra* (Alicante: Instituto de Estudios Alicantinos, 1973), pp. 159–61, 173–86.

10. M.D. van Biervliet d'Overbroeck, *"La voluntad* y *Antonio Azorín:* Reconsideración de su cronología," *American Hispanist* 2 (October 1976): 7.

11. On this polemic, see E. Inman Fox's introduction to *Antonio Azorín* (Barcelona: Labor, 1970), pp. 18–26; Valverde, pp. 218–20; and Biervliet d'Overbroeck, pp. 6–8.

12. In his edition of *Antonio Azorín* (p. 26), Fox argues that *Diary of a Sick Man, Will* and *Antonio Azorín* constitute a trilogy and that *The Confessions* opens the cycle of works which are collections of sketches: *Los pueblos, España,* and *Castilla.*

13. Two sketches of Azorín's mother and one of his father were added to later editions. See II, 89–91.

14. For a comparison of Cervantes's and Azorín's versions, see Marguerite C. Rand, *"El licenciado Vidriera,* Created by Cervantes, Recreated by Azorín," *Hispania* 37 (1954): 141–51.

15. For an analysis of motifs found in *Tomás Rueda,* see Gonzalo Sobejano, "Azorín el separado (Retablo de *Tomás Rueda*)," *Cuadernos Hispanoamericanos,* nos. 226–27 (October-November 1968): 239–65.

16. Azorín, *El licenciado Vidriera visto por Azorín* (Madrid: Residencia de Estudiantes, 1915), p. 155.

17. In large part this section on *Tomás Rueda* is an abridged version of my "The Narrator's Changing Perspective in Azorín's *Tomás Rueda," Revista de Estudios Hispánicos* 9 (1975): 343–57.

18. Martínez Cachero has used the word *franciscanismo* to describe the spirit of the novel. See pp. 181–85.

19. In a number of respects my discussion of *Doña Inés* coincides with that offered by Thomas C. Meehan in "El desdoblamiento interior en *Doña Inés,* de Azorín," *Cuadernos Hispanoamericanos,* no. 237 (September 1969): 644–68. Also useful are the following studies: Elena Catena de Vindel, "Lo azoriniano en *Doña Inés," Cuadernos Hispanoamericanos,* nos. 226–27 (October-November 1968): 266–91; Miguel Enguídanos, "Azorín en busca del tiempo divinal," *Papeles de Son Armadans* 15 (October 1959): 13–32; Julián Marías, *"Doña Inés," Insula,* no. 94 (October 15, 1953): 1, 9; Matías Montes Huidobro, "Un retrato de Azorín: Doña Inés," *Revista de Occidente,* no. 81 (December 1969): 362–72; Julian Palley, "Images of Time in *Doña Inés," Hispania* 54 (1971): 250–55; and José B. Vidal, "El tiempo a través de los personajes de *Doña Inés," Cuadernos Hispanoamericanos,* nos. 226–27 (October-November 1968): 220–38. In "Interior Duplication and the Problem of Form in the Modern Spanish Novel," *PMLA* 73 (1958): 393–406, Leon Livingstone comments on *Doña Inés* as an example of the temporal application of the concept of interior duplication.

20. Interwoven with the story is a description of how Don Pablo writes. The creative process, here described briefly, becomes the subject of Azorín's next novel, *El caballero inactual*.

21. At the time he wrote *Doña Inés*, Azorín apparently was not yet familiar with Proust's work. *Andando y pensando* (1929) contains an essay titled "El arte de Proust" (V, 176–80). See Lawrence D. Joiner's "The Portrayal of the Artist in Proust and Azorín," *Revista de Estudios Hispánicos* 10 (1976): 181–92.

22. The character Doña Inés also resembles Azorín. Her gaze is at times lost in the distance; at other moments it lovingly lingers over the surface of things. Like Azorín she is both drawn to and somewhat disdainful of the company of others, feeling herself part of the world and distant from it.

23. In Chapter 9 the life of Segovia over the centuries and the gradual decline of the woolen industry are symbolized by thousands of anonymous hands which slowly dissolve in a cinematic fade-out.

24. A modified repetition is also used in Chapter 5, where Doña Inés receives the letter in which Don Juan breaks off their relationship: "A letter is nothing and it is everything. . . .A letter is joy and it is sorrow. . . .A letter may bring good fortune and it may bring misfortune" (IV, 746).

25. According to legend, Macías met his death at the hands of a jealous husband. During the Romantic era the tragic story of the Galician troubadour was treated by Larra in the novel *El doncel de don Enrique el Doliente* and in the play *Macías*. Krause suggests (p. 247) that Azorín may have had Larra's novel in mind when he wrote *Doña Inés*.

Chapter Four

1. In a 1916 interview Azorín maintained that he had not lost the rebellious spirit of his youth, but he also described his present attitude as one of melancholy and mild pessimism regarding all the important problems of life. See Ramón Gómez de la Serna, *Azorín*, 3rd ed. (Buenos Aires: Losada, 1957), pp. 171, 172. Valverde uses the phrase "spiritual fatigue" (p. 331) to describe Azorín's new state of mind.

2. One of Azorín's less admirable traits is his propensity for dissociating himself from opinions he once fervently upheld. A reader unaware of Azorín's former concern with the decadence of Spain would be led by this "let us react" to assume that Azorín had never been "guilty" of speaking of decadence in connection with Spain. One of the most negative assessments of the works studied in this chapter is that of Blanco Aguinaga, who excoriates Azorín for abandoning his initially critical attitude toward Spain. See pp. 307–18 of *Juventud del 98*. Blanco Aguinaga regards

Azorín's *paisajismo* as escapism and accuses him of systematically falsifying the classics. It is true that Azorín interprets Spain and its literature in light of his own preoccupations and, by focusing on what is in accord with his own sensibility, presents a partial vision, but that vision has an aesthetic value which is independent of its political connotations.

3. The date 1905 is given by Manuel María Pérez López in *Azorín y la literatura española* (Salamanca: Univ. de Salamanca, 1974), p. 42.

4. *El político* (1908), a treatise on the attributes of the model politician, also sheds light on the evolution of Azorín's ideas. The politician, he declares, should not be afraid to rectify earlier positions, for an enthusiastic, naive youth of twenty and a mature man do not think the same way. (Azorín repeatedly maintained that there was nothing dishonorable about changing one's opinions, as long as the changes were sincere and disinterested. See, for example, IX, 1187.) The ardor of youth, he explains, makes us impetuous and inclines us to peremptory actions, but as years pass we learn that time resolves many conflicts. Azorín's new political stance is reflected in his statement that the politician should not attempt to change everything overnight. Rather, he should proceed slowly and cautiously, seeking innovation within a framework of order (II, 408–409).

5. As is the case with many of Azorín's books, *Towns* is a compilation of articles which had already been published in the press.

6. See Krause, pp. 202–208, 262, 270–71, and James H. Abbott, *Azorín y Francia* (Madrid: Seminarios y Ediciones, 1973), pp. 158–76.

7. This sketch, published in *España*, January 20, 1905, was not included in the original edition of *Towns*.

8. In *A Dream of Arcadia: Anti-Industrialism in Spanish Literature, 1895–1905* (Austin: Univ. of Texas Press, 1975), Lily Litvak studies five key manifestations of antiindustrialism: the appreciation of handicrafts, the revulsion against the modern city, the attraction to unsophisticated rural societies, the return to nature, and the interest in medieval times. See pp. 47–55, 80–87, 133–44, 176–83, 228–36, and her "Azorín's Anti-Urban Philosophy," *Revista de Estudios Hispánicos* 10 (1976): 283–96.

9. On the distinction between the real author and the implied author, i.e., the second self created in a literary work, see Wayne C. Booth, *The Rhetoric of Fiction* (Chicago: Univ. of Chicago Press, 1961), pp. 70–76.

10. The last word of the Spanish text, *espejo*, can be translated as "model" or as "mirror." Presumably the first meaning was the one Azorín had in mind, but the alternate meaning is also possible, for in this book Don Quixote is a mirror in which Azorín sees himself reflected.

11. H. Ramsden, ed., *La ruta de Don Quijote* (Manchester: Manchester Univ. Press, 1966), p. 160. Ramsden has also drawn attention to the inconsistencies evident in *The Route*.

12. The article bearing this title was published in *España* in 1904 and is reminiscent of Larra's "Vuelva usted mañana."

13. For the most part, the sketches included in *Spain* had appeared in the weekly *Blanco y Negro* during the preceding three years.

14. For a commentary on this sketch, see Eduardo Martínez de Pisón, "Un texto geográfico. 'En la montaña', de Azorín," in *El comentario de textos*, 2nd ed. (Madrid: Castalia, 1973), pp. 420–35.

15. Juan Manuel Rozas, ed., *Castilla* (Barcelona: Labor, 1973), pp. 22–32. The ensuing discussion follows Rozas's grouping of the sketches and his summary description of the unifying theme of each of the four sections.

16. Commenting in 1914 on Eugenio Noel's crusade against the bullfight and *flamenquismo* (II, 1109–17), Azorín notes that the mistaken concept of valor which is reflected in the *corrida* is particularly pernicious because it has spread to other spheres of life.

17. The blind writer, typifying essentialized vision, is a repeated figure in Azorín's narratives.

18. In the poem "A José María Palacio," written in Baeza in 1913, Machado makes similar use of sensory impressions, questions, exclamations, and future tenses which express conjecture about the present. On the basis of recollections of former springs shared with his wife Leonor, the poet visualizes the arrival of a new spring in Soria.

19. Barja, p. 264.

20. See E. Inman Fox, "Lectura y literatura (En torno a la inspiración libresca de Azorín)," *Cuadernos Hispanoamericanos*, no. 205 (January 1967): 5–26. *Un pueblecito (Riofrío de Avila)* (1916) is, as Fox notes (p. 11), an excellent example of the importance of other writers' work as a source of material for Azorín. At the annual book fair in Madrid he happens upon a copy of *Sentimientos patrióticos o conversaciones cristianas*, published in 1791 by Jacinto Bejarano Galavis y Nidos. Twenty-five of the sixty-five pages of *Un pueblecito* consist of Azorín's transcription of Bejarano's description of the geography, history, people, daily life, and customs of Riofrío de Avila. Bejarano is a man after Azorín's own heart, "a little Montaigne" (III, 537). Ironic, skeptical about many of the beliefs accepted by the villagers, sensitive, well read, and receptive to those foreign ideas which are compatible with the national spirit, Bejarano could also be termed an eighteenth-century Azorín. As a writer Bejarano, too, values clarity, regarding obscurity of style as the result of obscurity of thought. In commenting on Bejarano's ideas Azorín offers his own formula for attaining simplicity: *"place one thing after another"* (III, 546). *Un pueblecito* was the immediate inspiration for the essay "Azorín o primores de lo vulgar" in which Ortega points out that sensibility is Azorín's guide in his approach to history; he is *un sensitivo* rather than a philosopher of history (p. 158).

21. Of the volumes of literary criticism published between 1916 and 1935, the following are the most important: *Rivas y Larra*, 1916, *El paisaje de España visto por los españoles*, 1917, *Los dos Luises y otros*

ensayos, 1921 (studies on Golden Age writers, particularly Fray Luis de Granada and Fray Luis de León), *De Granada a Castelar*, 1922 (in which Azorín traces the evolution of the Spanish language), and *Lope en silueta*, 1935. A number of the books published in the postwar period consist of articles written over many years and compiled by José García Mercadal and Angel Cruz Rueda. Information as to the date and origin of the articles is often lacking. Poetry criticism is collected in *Leyendo a los poetas*, 1945, and drama criticism in *La farándula*, 1945, *Escena y sala*, 1947, and *Ante las candilejas*, 1947. *El artista y el estilo*, 1946, is a collection of articles on literary theory and style. Volumes concentrating on a single author's work include *Ante Baroja*, 1946, *Con Cervantes*, 1947, and *Con permiso de los cervantistas*, 1948. *La cabeza de Castilla*, 1950, contains articles on Burgos and the Cid. More heterogeneous are *Los clásicos redivivos*. *Los clásicos futuros*, 1945, *El oasis de los clásicos*, 1952, and *A voleo*, 1954. For a study of the first of these last three collections, see M.D. van Biervliet d'Overbroeck, "*Los clásicos redivivos*: Azorín's Attempt to Revivify His Presentation of the Classics," *Revista de Estudios Hispánicos* 11 (1977): 411–23. Of the works not included in the *Obras completas*, *Escritores*, 1956, contains some interesting studies on nineteenth- and twentieth-century novelists, as does *Crítica de años cercanos*, 1967, on contemporary writers. Since the publication of the *Obras completas*—a complete misnomer—some thirty additional books have appeared, most of which are collections of Azorín's newspaper articles. For a listing, see Sáinz de Bujanda, pp. 220–39.

22. This in no way means that Azorín is not knowledgeable about the scholarly analyses of other critics but that such material is often simply not relevant to his purpose. Erudition can be a useful tool, but for Azorín it is not an aim in itself. Revealing is his criticism of Menéndez y Pelayo's studies for being erudite and enumerative rather than internal, interpretive, and psychological (II, 899).

23. See II, 631–34, 905–906. On the subject of Azorín's reactions to Galdós's play *Electra*, see E. Inman Fox, "Galdós' *Electra*: A Detailed Study of Its Historical Significance and the Polemic between Martínez Ruiz and Maeztu," *Anales Galdosianos* 1 (1966): 131–41.

24. For detailed analyses of Azorín's literary criticism, see E. Inman Fox, *Azorín as a Literary Critic* (New York: Hispanic Institute, 1962), and Pérez López, *Azorín y la literatura española*. The second of these books contains a useful index to Azorín's essays on some 175 authors.

25. See, for example, his "act of contrition" with respect to Valera (III, 1200–1201).

26. On the evolution of Azorín's ideas concerning intelligence and will, action and contemplation, see Livingstone, *Tema y forma*, pp. 143–68.

27. Also see II, 1148–63.

28. The subjectivity which characterizes Azorín's literary criticism also

marks his approach to landscape. In *El paisaje de España visto por los españoles* he writes: "There is in our sense of landscape . . . a purely subjective element" (III, 1160). Many of his descriptions of the *paisaje* of Spain are based not on direct observation but on his recollections and reading or are creations of his imagination. Even when direct observation is his starting point, Azorín increasingly tends to poetically transform visible reality and imbue it with his own emotions. He insists that "we ourselves are the landscape; the landscape is our spirit, its melancholies, its moments of placidity, its yearnings, its misfortunes. A modern aesthetician has maintained that the landscape does not exist until it is portrayed in painting or in literature. Only then—when it is created in art—do we in reality begin to see the landscape. What in reality we then see is what the artist has created with his inspiration" (III, 1171). Regarding Azorín's treatment of landscape, see Marguerite C. Rand, *Castilla en Azorín* (Madrid: Revista de Occidente, 1956); Carola Reig, "El paisaje en Azorín," *Cuadernos Hispanoamericanos*, no. 65 (May 1955): 206–22; and Rosa Seeleman, "The Treatment of Landscape in the Novelists of the Generation of 1898," *Hispanic Review* 4 (1936): 226–38.

29. By 1924 Azorín's assessment is quite different. In *An Hour in the Life of Spain* he describes the classic theater as "a synthesis of all Spanish life" (IV, 523) and asserts that of necessity certain aspects of everyday life are excluded from this theater. After all, if the dramatist were "to stoop" to such details or justify the entrances and exits of his characters, his work would descend from the elevated plane on which he wishes to place it. Errors and anachronisms are of no significance. What is important is "the tone of dignity, grandeur, and elevation above everyday realities" (IV, 524) of the characters.

30. A less negative appraisal of Quevedo's work is found in *Marginal Notes on the Classics* (III, 235–46).

Chapter Five

1. In *La deshumanización del arte e ideas sobre la novela* (1925), Ortega y Gasset called attention to the decline of the novel.

2. Azorín singles out for special attention Henri-René Lenormand, Jean-Victor Pellerin, Gantillon, and Jean-Jacques Bernard. Regarding Pirandellian themes in these dramatists' plays, see Thomas Bishop, *Pirandello and the French Theater* (New York: New York Univ. Press, 1960).

3. Granell is among those who consider these works Expressionistic.

4. For the purposes of the present study, the provenance of a particular technique or type of imagery is less important than the use to which it is put by Azorín. For an analysis of Impressionism, Symbolism, Expressionism, Cubism, and Surrealism as they relate to his works, see Robert E. Lott, *The Structure and Style of Azorín's* El caballero inactual (Athens: Univ. of Georgia Press, 1963), pp. 4-16. Lott states that during his experi-

mental period Azorín "successfully fuses new elements and techniques with his customary style, which is basically impressionistic-symbolistic" (p. 16).

5. *Dictionary of World Literary Terms*, ed. Joseph T. Shipley (Boston: The Writer, Inc., 1970), pp. 319–20.

6. Martínez Cachero, p. 210.

7. Anna Balakian, *Surrealism: The Road to the Absolute* (New York: Noonday Press, 1959), p. 109. Further differences are noted by Lott: "In Azorín there are no iconoclastic attempts to shock, nor an involvement in politics, nor the heavy sensualism characteristic of French surrealism" ("Azorín's Experimental Period and Surrealism," PMLA 79 [1964]: 307). For additional background on Surrealism in France and Spain, see Georges Lemaître, *From Cubism to Surrealism in French Literature*, rev. ed. (Cambridge: Harvard Univ. Press, 1947), and C.B. Morris, *Surrealism and Spain: 1920-1936* (Cambridge: Cambridge Univ. Press, 1972).

8. In *El libro de Levante* Azorín insists that the writer should not become entangled in a forest of details; rather, he should throw himself into the soul of things (V, 392).

9. Quoted in Martínez Cachero, p. 211.

10. Félix seeks solitude in order to refine his sensibility, but he realizes that there is a point at which solitude and renunciation of the world might become counterproductive. He might lose all naturalness and become "inebriated by his own sensibility" (V, 104).

11. Lott notes that this passage is reminiscent of Rainer Maria Rilke *(Structure and Style*, p. 74).

12. Lott, *Structure and Style*, p. 26.

13. Lott writes that "there is still a tightly woven intellectual organization beneath the juxtaposed phrases...and the chaotic worlds of the subconscious and of oneiric experience, as a rule, are only hinted at" *(Structure and Style*, p. 69).

14. Regarding the use of verbless sentences and infinitives in the novel, see Lott, *Structure and Style*, pp. 61–65.

15. Félix Vargas is also the protagonist of six stories. See Lott, *Structure and Style*, pp. 77–82. Azorín's collections of short stories have been studied by Mirella d'Ambrosio Servodidio, *Azorín: Escritor de cuentos* (New York: Las Américas, 1971), and by Mariano Baquero Goyanes, "Los cuentos de Azorín," *Cuadernos Hispanoamericanos*, nos. 226–27 (October-November 1968): 355-74.

16. Livingstone, "Self-creation and Alienation," p. 7.

17. Ibid., p. 25.

18. Because of its deliberate incompleteness, *The Book of the Levant* is also an antinovel. "When unattainment of form...is adopted as an intentional esthetic, that is to say, when incompleteness is a purposeful artistic tenet, the prenovel becomes an anti-novel" (Livingstone, "The 'Esthetic

of Repose,' " p. 243). In *The Book of the Levant* the author speaks of the attraction of what is indefinite. He enjoys the "voluptuous" sensation of being able to do something and yet not doing it, the interval when we hesitate between sleep and wakefulness, the "consoling lapse" between the moment when one image has been discarded and another not yet adopted. Azorín's preference for intermediate states is also apparent in the frequency with which he uses the word *penumbra* (semidarkness, half-light) and describes threshold scenes, as at the end of *The Timeless Gentleman*.

19. The two images are somewhat reminiscent of the worlds of Julie Récamier and Santa Teresa. Several of the motifs of *The Timeless Gentleman* reappear in *The Book of the Levant*. In Chapter 35 of the first work, Félix leaves Biarritz and returns to Spain. The image of Andrea's hand waving good-bye is linked with an awareness of the passing of time and with the idea of renunciation. The farewell scene brings to Félix's mind the vision of a fourteenth-century gentleman who has renounced the world for the four walls of a monastery cell. The image of "el caballero en la celda" is more fully developed in the 1929 novel, as is that of a hand resting on the latch of a door.

20. Azorín's use of angels may have been inspired by his reading of Rilke, but a more immediate influence would appear to be that of Rafael Alberti. *The Book of the Levant* was written during the months of August and September 1929. On June 6 of that year Azorín published an encomiastic review of *Sobre los ángeles*. (The review is contained in *Crítica de años cercanos*, ed. José García Mercadal [Madrid: Taurus, 1967], pp. 75–78.) Profoundly impressed by the book, Azorín declares that in it Alberti has gone beyond the sphere of the world of forms and the anecdotal, ascending into the realm of the impalpable. The poet has revealed a new world in which past and future seem to have been cut away, leaving us with a pure present. Azorín also enumerates the hierarchies of angels beloved by Alberti, expanding on this enumeration in Chapter 6 of *The Book of the Levant*. In a second article, published in *La Prensa* on September 8 and included in *Ultramarinos*, ed. José García Mercadal (Barcelona: Edhasa, 1966), pp. 112–18, Azorín wrote of the "irreducible" poetry of Guillén, Salinas, and Alberti, poetry in which reality has been purified, refined, and essentialized. During his experimental period Azorín evinces a similar interest in reducing the world to its elemental components and seeing it in terms of color, lines, and light.

21. On the limitations of the intellect, see V, 400. Subsequently the author quotes a passage from a theological work to the effect that although reason cannot penetrate to the core of mysteries, it can illuminate them by pointing out the similarities they bear to things of the natural order.

22. The author observes that there is a world of sounds which is inaudible to the human ear, a world of colors and rays of light which is

invisible to the eye, i.e., a reality which lies beyond human perception. References to acoustics, optics, photographic processes, and laboratories are frequent during Azorín's experimental period.

23. Thinking about Monóvar, the author feels linked to the chain of ancestors who over the centuries have created Spain. But this feeling of continuity is counterbalanced by an awareness of the effect of the passage of time, as seen in the account of the gradual disappearance of the conservatives who once gathered in the local casino. With the death of the last of their members, an entire world of anecdotes, episodes, and memories fades into oblivion. In comparison with the history of the universe, the history of the city, as well as that of Spain, is but a "flash of lightning in eternity" (V, 423).

24. The philosophical implications of the autonomous character have been analyzed by Joseph E. Gillet, "The Autonomous Character in Spanish and European Literature," *Hispanic Review* 24 (1956): 179–90, and by Livingstone, "Interior Duplication," pp. 393–406. Livingstone interprets the use of autonomous characters and the technique of interior duplication as expressions of a relativistic metaphysic according to which reality and imagination, fact and fiction, life and art are not mutually exclusive but equivalent and interchangeable. On Unamuno's *Niebla*, one of the most provocative statements of this metaphysic, see pp. 400–401.

25. In gratitude for this paean, which constitutes approximately half the novel, the citizens of Monóvar honored Azorín in February 1930, and hundreds of copies of his novel were distributed in schools in the province of Alicante.

26. Regarding Azorín's use of cinematic techniques, see Robert E. Lott, "Considerations on Azorín's Literary Techniques and the Other Arts," *Kentucky Romance Quarterly* 18 (1971): 423–34. During the 1950s Azorín's interest in the cinema intensified. See his *El cine y el momento* (Madrid: Biblioteca Nueva, 1953) and *El efímero cine* (Madrid: Afrodisio Aguado, 1955).

27. Also see Chapters 27 and 34.

28. The dog resembles Berganza in Cervantes's *El coloquio de los perros*.

29. As in *Will*, intelligence is conceived as dissociative; it entails a recognition of irremediable limitation and thus leads to suffering. It is in the first section of the epilogue that Azorín comes closest to Surrealism, but he does not totally forego logic. A rationale for the dream is furnished in a reference to incidents which occurred during wakefulness and involved *un depósito* and *la llamita de un soplete*, the key images of the subsequent dream. See Lott, "Azorín's Experimental Period and Surrealism," p. 314.

30. Great attention is paid to lighting effects and different forms of light: sunlight, moonlight, starlight, subdued light, half-light, vivid light, streaks and pools of light, electric light, lantern light, lamplight,

candlelight, firelight, the cold light of cruelty, and the warm light of compassion.

31. Lott, "Azorín's Experimental Period and Surrealism," p. 314.

32. See Malcolm D. van Biervliet d'Overbroeck, "Azorín's *Comedia del arte* and *Angelita: auto sacramental*: Two Misunderstood Titles, Two Misunderstood Plays," *Journal of Spanish Studies: Twentieth Century* 5 (1977): 47–55.

33. Livingstone, "Interior Duplication," p. 405. See note 24. The device of the play-within-a-play or the novel-within-a-novel, both forms of interior duplication, enables the writer to demonstrate the interaction and reversibility of reality and fiction.

34. The role of the author was played by Azorín when the trilogy was performed in Madrid in 1928. (Each of the plays had been performed separately during 1927.) Despite Azorín's declaration that his reading of Rilke's *The Notebooks of Malte Laurids Brigge* led him to write the trilogy (IV, 1036), it owes more to Maeterlinck. See Frederick S. Stimson, "*Lo invisible*: Azorín's Debt to Maeterlinck," *Hispanic Review* 26 (1958): 64–70.

35. Azorín's other plays include "Judit" (1926), which was not performed or published, *La guerrilla* (1936), and *Farsa docente* (1942). *El Clamor* (1928), a satire of the newspaper world written in collaboration with Muñoz Seca, resulted in Azorín's being expelled from the Press Association. During 1926 and 1927 he had published a number of articles criticizing the unintelligence, insensitivity, and general ineptitude of drama critics, many of whom were less than enthusiastic about Azorín's own plays. His attacks, obviously, did not endear him to the critics. On Azorín's theater, see Lott, "Azorín's Experimental Period and Surrealism," pp. 308–10; Guillermo Díaz-Plaja, "El teatro de Azorín," *Cuadernos de Literatura Contemporánea*, nos. 16–17 (1945): 369–87; Lawrence Anthony LaJohn, *Azorín and the Spanish Stage* (New York: Hispanic Institute, 1961); Wilma Newberry, *The Pirandellian Mode in Spanish Literature from Cervantes to Sastre* (Albany: State Univ. of New York Press, 1973), pp. 97–115; and the articles contained in the commemorative issue dedicated to Azorín by *Cuadernos Hispanoamericanos*, nos. 226–27 (October-November 1968): E. Inman Fox, "La campaña teatral de Azorín (Experimentalismo, Evreinoff e *Ifach*)," pp. 375–89; Ricardo Doménech, "Azorín, dramaturgo," pp. 390–405; Olga Kattan, "*La guerrilla* de Azorín: Hacia una interpretación," pp. 406-12.

Chapter Six

1. The first forty-five chapters of *Memorias inmemoriales* were published in 1943 under the title *Memorias*.

2. Azorín notes that in later years there was a cooling of the friendship which he and Blasco Ibáñez once enjoyed, implying that the rupture was

due to the fact that they held contrasting views of art. In actuality, political differences separated the two men. In 1915 Blasco, a confirmed revolutionary, reproached Azorín for having abandoned his initial progressivism. See Valverde, pp. 29–31.

3. Azorín succinctly described the subject of his novel as the contrast between a prewar and a postwar writer (quoted in Martínez Cachero, pp. 252–53). Dávila is modeled on Dionisio Ridruejo, to whom *The Writer* is dedicated. See Martínez Cachero, p. 253, and Livingstone, *Tema y. forma*, pp. 158–59, n. 186.

4. Quoted in Martínez Cachero, p. 250, n. 12.

5. In view of Azorín's preoccupation with the effects of age, the description of Quiroga's friend Sixto Prendes is especially significant. At seventy-six Prendes leads a restricted existence, but he is in full possession of his faculties and well informed about current literature.

6. Subsequently Dávila returns to the subject of Quiroga's past, describing it as an honorable one of study and love for Spain. During the early postwar years Azorín, as a member of the Generation of 1898 and a onetime supporter of the Second Republic, was viewed with suspicion by the more doctrinaire elements of the Right. In *The Writer* he in effect affirms that neither the validity of his literary work nor his patriotism can be questioned, and he figuratively declares his adhesion to the Franco regime. In Chapter 31 Quiroga addresses the group of young men who gather at Dávila's house and urges them to work for Spain with abnegation and perseverance. At the end of his exhortation he cries, "¡En pie y arriba España!" (VI, 384), and his listeners leap to their feet, raise their arms in the Falangist salute, and shout, "¡Arriba España!" In an interview published in November 1941 Azorín defended his generation, saying that even though it was politically ineffective, it provided the "leaven" for the action of the current generation (quoted in Martínez Cachero, p. 252). Quiroga tells his listeners that they represent thought allied with action.

7. Dávila's interest in asceticism is prefigured in Chapter 14 of the *Annals* when Quiroga tells a friend that he is writing a novel about a cultured man who leads an ascetic life not in the wilderness but in the midst of a populous city. (The friend's name is Pedro Chaide, a clear evocation of the sixteenth-century ascetic Pedro Malón de Chaide.) Quiroga's words suggest, or at least do not preclude, the possibility that the work to which he refers is not *El escritor* but a new novel and that it too has Dávila as its protagonist.

8. Leon Livingstone, "The Pursuit of Form in the Novels of Azorín," *PMLA* 77 (1962): 127.

9. In Víctor's mind, people he once knew, characters from his novels, physicians about whom he has read, and the three local doctors who successively attend him are all equally real or unreal.

10. Víctor, along with Doña Inés and Don Pablo, is analyzed by Fran-

cisco Marco Merenciano in *Fronteras de la locura: Tres personajes de Azorín vistos por un psiquiatra* (Valencia: Metis, 1947). On the relationship between creativity and health, see Livingstone's "Self-creation and Alienation," pp. 7, 25, 37–38.

11. Livingstone, "The Pursuit of Form," p. 132.

12. The author cites the *Quixote* as an example of the fusion of reality and fantasy. The prologue's title calls to mind Pirandello's *Così è (se vi pare)*. Madariaga suggests that Parts I and II of *Capriccio* could be titled "Ten Characters in Search of a Solution" (p. 169).

13. José Carlos Mainer writes that the provisionality and contradictoriness of the novel are a metaphor for the incoherence and indetermination of the world ("Para un análisis formal de *Capricho* y *La isla sin aurora*," *Insula*, no. 246 [May 1967]: 5).

14. The idea that the literary critic and the author are mirror images of one another is illustrated in a brief scene in which the author joins the critic in the indeterminate and the two sit and gaze at one another. The author wonders "who is the critic and who the author?" (VI, 904).

15. Several other characters share Azorín's preoccupations and personal experiences. The septuagenarian manager writes concisely and has a passion for words; the financial editor fondly recalls his years in Paris; and the art critic remembers Rembrandt's paintings in the Louvre, paintings which Azorín frequently mentioned in the stories he wrote while in exile.

16. Before sending his creations out into the world, the author urges them to bear in mind that their future life depends on what they now decide to do. The scene is reminiscent of Calderón's *El gran teatro del mundo*.

17. Granell (pp. 199–200, 204–208) applies Franz Roh's term "magic realism" to Azorín's last works. On the appropriateness of the term with reference to *La isla sin aurora*, see Robert E. Lott's "Sobre el método narrativo y el estilo en las novelas de Azorín," *Cuadernos Hispanoamericanos*, nos. 226–27 (October-November 1968): 209–11.

18. On Azorín's conception of the novel as a hybrid form lying midway between pure poetry and the literal realism of the theater, see Livingstone, "The Pursuit of Form," pp. 125–27.

19. With its emphasis on moral philosophy and the education of the individual, *The Island without Dawn* is reminiscent of Gracián's *Oráculo manual y arte de prudencia* and *El criticón*. Lott points to the influence on Azorín's novel of Lucian's fantastic, satiric *True History* ("Sobre el método narrativo," p. 209).

20. The story of Serrano, who was shipwrecked in the Caribbean in the sixteenth century, was related by the Inca Garcilaso de la Vega in his *Comentarios reales*, published in 1609.

21. Livingstone, "The Pursuit of Form," p. 133. Livingstone is here referring to *María Fontán* and *Salvadora de Olbena*. See *Tema y forma*, pp. 98–99, 214.

22. See Andrés Amorós, *Sociología de una novela rosa* (Madrid: Taurus, 1968).

23. In "Spatial Form in Modern Literature," *Sewanee Review* 53 (1945): 221–40, 433–56, 643–53, Joseph Frank points out that by breaking up temporal sequence the novelist seeks to escape the limits imposed upon him by the "time-logic" of language. By appropriating the techniques of the visual arts and juxtaposing elements in space rather than presenting them as proceeding through time, he can convey the sense of simultaneous activity occurring in different places. This is what Azorín has done in the initial chapters of *Salvadora*. His eyes and ears have registered a multitude of sensations which have been recorded on paper, one after another, but they have all been perceived at the same moment. Frank notes (p. 234) that a novel such as *Ulysses* must be read as if it were a modern poem; fragments must be fitted together and allusions kept in mind until, by reflexive reference, they can be linked to their complements. The description of Olbena must be read in the same way.

24. Livingstone comments that "the declaration of Ontiveros establishes the relative functions of reality and the ideal in the creation of the work of art. Reality is the necessary starting point of the artist, and the firmer the interpretation of reality the firmer will be the structure which the artist elaborates. But this reality is always an interpretation, a hypothesis...so that art can never be only the copy of reality, but is always its creation" ("The Pursuit of Form," p. 132).

25. It is fitting that the last word in the "history" of Salvadora is delivered by the houses of Olbena and the garden of Salvadora's home. Addressing the author, they explain that they have influenced Salvadora's character and have witnessed her changing moods. Their portrait of her has the poetic truth which makes fiction superior to history.

26. For a more detailed study of *Salvadora*, see Lawrence D. Joiner and Joseph W. Zdenek, "*Salvadora de Olbena*: A 'Summa' of Azorín's Artistic Credo," *Research Studies* 44 (1976): 111–19, and my "Azorín's *Salvadora de Olbena*: Reality and the Artist," *Hispanófila*, no. 56 (1976): 53–62.

Chapter Seven

1. Livingstone, "The Pursuit of Form," p. 133.

2. On Azorín's anticipation of certain features of the *nouveau roman*, see Antonio Risco, "La novela de Azorín y el 'Nouveau Roman' francés," *Revista Canadiense de Estudios Hispánicos* 1 (1976): 75–98. Such recent works as Luis Goytisolo's *Los verdes de mayo hasta el mar* (1976) and Torrente Ballester's *Fragmentos de apocalipsis* (1977) are but two examples of the resurgence of interest in the self-conscious novel.

Selected Bibliography

PRIMARY SOURCES

A Selective Listing of Works by Azorín (arranged chronologically):
El alma castellana (1600-1800). Madrid: Librería Internacional, 1900.
Diario de un enfermo. Madrid: Establecimiento tipográfico de Ricardo Fe, 1901.
La voluntad. Barcelona: Henrich y Cía., 1902.
Antonio Azorín. Madrid: Viuda de Rodríguez Serra, 1903.
Las confesiones de un pequeño filósofo. Madrid: Librería de Fernando Fe, 1904.
Los pueblos. Madrid: Leonardo Williams, 1905.
La ruta de Don Quijote. Madrid: Leonardo Williams, 1905.
España. Madrid: Librería de Francisco Beltrán, 1909.
Lecturas españolas. Madrid: Imprenta de là Revista de Archivos, 1912.
Castilla. Madrid: Imprenta de la Revista de Archivos, 1912.
Clásicos y modernos. Madrid: Renacimiento, 1913.
Los valores literarios. Madrid: Renacimiento, 1914.
Al margen de los clásicos. Madrid: Residencia de Estudiantes, 1915.
El licenciado Vidriera visto por Azorín (Tomás Rueda). Madrid: Residencia de Estudiantes, 1915.
Un pueblecito (Riofrío de Avila). Madrid: Residencia de Estudiantes, 1916.
El paisaje de España visto por los españoles. Madrid: Renacimiento, 1917.
Don Juan. Madrid: Caro Raggio, 1922.
Una hora de España (Entre 1560 y 1590). Madrid: Caro Raggio, 1924.
Doña Inés. Madrid: Caro Raggio, 1925.
Félix Vargas (El caballero inactual). Madrid: Biblioteca Nueva, 1928.
Superrealismo (El libro de Levante). Madrid: Biblioteca Nueva, 1929.
Pueblo. Madrid: Biblioteca Nueva, 1930.
Madrid. Madrid: Biblioteca Nueva, 1941.
El escritor. Madrid: Espasa-Calpe, 1942.
El enfermo. Madrid: Adán, 1943.
Capricho. Madrid: Espasa-Calpe, 1943.
La isla sin aurora. Barcelona: Destino, 1944.
María Fontán. Madrid: Espasa-Calpe, 1944.
Salvadora de Olbena. Zaragoza: Cronos, 1944.
Memorias inmemoriales. Madrid: Biblioteca Nueva, 1946.

Obras completas. Ed. Angel Cruz Rueda. 9 vols. Madrid: Aguilar, 1947–1954; 2nd ed., 1959–1963.
For bibliographic details regarding other works, see Sáinz de Bujanda, Fernando. *Clausura de un centenario: Guía bibliográfica de Azorín*. Madrid: Revista de Occidente, 1974.

SECONDARY SOURCES

The following listing of some twenty of the most important studies on Azorín is intended as the briefest of introductions to the wealth of critical material available. References to many additional studies may be found in the notes.

BARJA, CÉSAR. "Azorín." In *Libros y autores contemporáneos*. New York: G.E. Stechert & Co., 1935, pp. 264–98. Contains valuable insights into Azorín's obsession with time.

CLAVERÍA, CARLOS. "Sobre el tema del tiempo en Azorín." In *Cinco estudios de literatura española moderna*. Salamanca: Consejo Superior de Investigaciones Científicas, 1945, pp. 49–67. Points out the influence of the ideas of Jean Marie Guyau on Azorín's concept of time.

FOX, E. INMAN. *Azorín as a Literary Critic*. New York: Hispanic Institute, 1962. A highly favorable appraisal.

————. "Lectura y literatura (En torno a la inspiración libresca de Azorín)." *Cuadernos Hispanoamericanos*, no. 205 (January 1967): 5–26. Excellent discussion of the importance of other writers' work as a source of inspiration for Azorín.

GRANELL, MANUEL. *Estética de Azorín*. Madrid: Biblioteca Nueva, 1949. Traces the evolution of Azorín's vision of reality and his treatment of time and space.

GRANJEL, LUIS S. *Retrato de Azorín*. Madrid: Guadarrama, 1958. An objective biography.

KRAUSE, ANNA. *Azorín, the Little Philosopher: Inquiry into the Birth of a Literary Personality*. Univ. of California Publications in Modern Philology, vol. 28, no. 4. Berkeley: Univ. of California Press, 1948. Focuses on Azorín's early intellectual development.

LAÍN ENTRALGO, PEDRO. *La generación del noventa y ocho*. 3rd ed. Madrid: Espasa-Calpe, 1956. Classic study of the *noventayochistas*.

LIVINGSTONE, LEON. "Self-creation and Alienation in the Novels of Azorín." *Journal of Spanish Studies: Twentieth Century* 1 (1973): 5–43. Examines the relationships among creativity, identity, and mental disturbance.

————. *Tema y forma en las novelas de Azorín*. Madrid: Gredos, 1970. A fundamental work which includes revised versions of Livingstone's articles on interior duplication, the pursuit of form in Azorín's novels, the "esthetic of repose" in *Diario de un enfermo*, the theme of intelligence and will, and the problem of time.

LOTT, ROBERT E. "Azorín's Experimental Period and Surrealism." *PMLA* 79 (1964): 305–20. An overview of the novels, short stories, and plays published between 1926 and 1931. Lott demonstrates that these works cannot properly be termed Surrealistic.

————. *The Structure and Style of Azorín's* El caballero inactual. Athens: Univ. of Georgia Press, 1963. Perceptive analysis of Azorín's 1928 novel.

MADARIAGA, PILAR DE. "Las novelas de Azorín: Estudio de sus temas y de su técnica." Diss. Middlebury College 1949. A thorough and discerning examination of Azorín's novels.

MARAVALL, JOSÉ ANTONIO. "Azorín. Idea y sentido de la microhistoria." *Cuadernos Hispanoamericanos*, nos. 226–27 (October-November 1968): 28–77. An illuminating essay.

MARTÍNEZ CACHERO, JOSÉ MARÍA. *Las novelas de Azorín*. Madrid: Insula, 1960. Good discussion of Azorín's novelistic theory and practice.

ORTEGA Y GASSET, JOSÉ. "Azorín o primores de lo vulgar." In *Obras completas*. Vol. II. Madrid: Revista de Occidente, 1946, 153–85. The best of the early commentaries on Azorín, first published in 1917.

PÉREZ LÓPEZ, MANUEL MARÍA. *Azorín y la literatura española*. Salamanca: Univ. de Salamanca, 1974. A comprehensive review of Azorín's essays on Spanish literature and a balanced assessment of his strengths and weaknesses as a critic.

VALVERDE, JOSÉ MARÍA. *Azorín*. Barcelona: Planeta, 1971. A good survey of Azorín's life and works, with particular emphasis on the 1893–1905 years and his journalistic articles.

Index

Abbott, James H., 145n6
ABC, 18, 20, 21, 76
Alarcón, Pedro Antonio de, 85
Alas, Leopoldo, 26, 85, 140nll, 141nl
Alberti, Rafael, 86, 150n20; *Sobre los ángeles*, 150n20
Alomar, Gabriel, 92
Amadis of Gaul, 33
Amat y Maestre, Miguel, 142–43n9
Amorós, Andrés, 142n3, 155n22
Arolas, Juan, 131
Arte Joven, 17
Austria, Don Juan de, 21
Aznar Cardura, Pedro, 89
Azorín (José Martínez Ruiz): life and times, 13–22
WORKS—MEMOIRS:
Madrid, 22, 114–15, 139n7
Memorias, 152nl
Memories of Time Immemorial (Memorias inmemoriales), 14–15, 20, 51, 114, 115, 129, 133–34
Paris, 114, 115
Valencia, 38, 114

WORKS—NOVELS:
Antonio Azorín, 18, 42–47, 52, 68, 73, 96
Book of the Levant, The (El libro de Levante), 102–106, 149n8
Capriccio (Capricho), 121–26, 129, 130, 133
Confessions of a Little Philosopher, The (Las confesiones de un pequeño filósofo), 15, 18, 47–51, 52, 67–68, 74, 96
Diary of a Sick Man (Diario de un enfermo), 18, 31, 34–36, 136

Don Juan, 55–58, 107
Doña Inés, 58–64, 96, 137, 140n20, 142ch2n6
Félix Vargas. See The Timeless Gentleman
Island without Dawn, The (La isla sin aurora), 126–29, 136
licenciado Vidriera visto por Azorín, El. See Tomás Rueda
María Fontán, 129–31, 136
People, The (Pueblo), 107–109
Salvadora de Olbena, 131–34, 136
Sick Man, The (El enfermo), 118–21
Superrealismo. See The Book of the Levant
Timeless Gentleman, The (El caballero inactual), 96–102, 106, 142ch2n6, 144n20, 150nn18–19
Tomás Rueda, 13, 51–55, 67, 125
Will (La voluntad), 18, 34, 37–42, 44–45, 46, 47, 48, 50, 51, 52, 70, 71, 72, 85, 87, 88, 96, 101–102, 136, 139n8, 151n29
Writer, The (El escritor), 86, 115–18

WORKS—PLAYS:
Angelita, 110
Brandy, Lots of Brandy (Brandy, mucho brandy), 110
Cervantes, or The Enchanted House (Cervantes, o La casa encantada), 111
Clamor, El, 152n35
Commedia dell'arte (Comedia del arte), 110
Doctor Death, de 3 a 5, 112–13
Farsa docente, 152n35
guerrilla, La, 152n35

Invisible, The (Lo invisible), 111–13
"Judit," 152n35
Old Spain!, 109
Power of Love, The (La fuerza del amor), 33–34
Reaper, The (El segador), 112
Spider on the Mirror, The (La arañita en el espejo), 112

WORKS—SHORTER PROSE WORKS:
Andando y pensando, 144n21
Ante Baroja, 147n21
Ante las candilejas, 147n21
"arte de Proust, El," 144n21
artista y el estilo, El, 147n21
"Atmosphere of Argamasilla, The" ("Ambiente de Argamasilla"), 72
A voleo, 147n21
Begging the Leave of Cervantists (Con permiso de los cervantistas), 83, 147n21
Bohemia, 29–30, 34
cabeza de Castilla, La, 147n21
Castile (Castilla), 23, 65, 76–82
"Castilian City, A" ("Una ciudad castellana"), 76
Castilian Soul, The (El alma castellana [1600–1800]), 32–33, 85, 141n4
"Cathedral, The" ("La catedral"), 77
Charivari, 28–29, 34
cine y el momento, El, 151n26
"City and a Balcony, A" ("Una ciudad y un balcón"), 24, 77, 81
clásicos redivivos. Los clásicos futuros, Los, 147n21
Classic and Modern Authors (Clásicos y modernos), 65, 86, 88–90
"Closed House, The" ("La Casa cerrada"), 80, 81
"Clouds, The" ("Las nubes"), 23–24, 78, 80
Con Cervantes, 147n21
Criminal Sociology (La sociología criminal), 31
Crítica de años cercanos, 147n21, 150n20
"Death of a Friend: Sarrió, The" ("La muerte de un amigo: Sarrió"), 68

De Granada a Castelar, 147n21
"Delicado (1530)," 75
"Disgust" ('Hastío"), 27
"Don José Nieto (1656)," 74–75
"Don Quixote, Vanquished" ("Don Quijote, vencido"), 125–26
dos Luises y otros ensayos, Los, 146–47n21
efímero cine, El, 151n26
"Elegy, An" ("Una elegía"), 69
"Epilogue in 1960" (Epílogo en 1960"), 70
Escena y sala, 147n21
Escritores, 147n21
Evolution of Criticism, The (La evolución de la crítica), 31
farándula, La, 147n21
Feeling Spain (Sintiendo a España), 20, 21
"Fiesta, The" ("La fiesta"), 70
"Flute in the Night, A" ("Una flauta en la noche"), 79, 80, 81
"Fragments from a Diary" ("Fragmentos de un diario"), 29
"Fragrance of the Glass, The" ("La fragancia del vaso"), 78
"Friend, The" ("El amigo"), 29
"Good Judge, The" ("El buen juez"), 68–69
"Hidalgo, A" ("Un hidalgo"), 69
hidalgos, Los, 141n4
Hour in the Life of Spain, An (Una hora de España [Entre 1560 y 1590]), 65–66, 148n29
"Ideals of Yesteryear, The" ("Los ideales de antaño"), 26–27
"Inevitable, The" ("Lo fatal"), 78
Landscapes" ("Paisajes"), 30
Leyendo a los poetas, 147n21
"Life, A" ("Una vida"), 29–30
"Life of a Poor Farmer, The" ("Vida de un labrantín"), 74
Literary Anarchists (Anarquistas literarios), 27, 85
Literary Criticism in Spain (La crítica literaria en España), 26, 32
Literary Values (Los valores literarios), 65, 86, 88, 90–92
Literature (Literatura), 27–28, 29
Lope en silueta, 147n21

Marginal Notes on the Classics (Al margen de los clásicos), 65, 92–93
"Master, The" ("El maestro"), 29
oasis de los cláscos, El, 147n21
"On the Mountain" ("En la montaña"), 76
paisaje de España visto por los españoles, El, 146n21, 148n28
"Parliamentary Impressions" ("Impresiones parlamentarias"), 18
"Past Time" ("El tiempo pasado"), 126
Pecuchet, Demagogue (Pecuchet, demagogo), 30–31
político, El, 145n4
"Psychological Process" ("Proceso psicologico"), 66
pueblecito (Riofrío de Avila), Un, 146n20
Rivas y Larra, 146n21
Route of Don Quixote, The (La ruta de Don Quijote), 19, 65, 70–73
"Sea, The" ("El mar"), 77–78, 81
"Small Red Light, A" ("Una lucecita roja"), 80, 81–82
Social Notes (Notas sociales) 27
Solitudes (Soledades), 30
"Some Hat Makers" ("Unas sombrereras [1520]"), 75
Spain (España), 65, 73–76, 96
Spaniards in Paris (Españoles en París), 20–21
Spanish Readings (Lecturas españolas), 65, 86–88
Squibs (Buscapiés), 26–27
Thinking about Spain (Pensando en España), 20, 21, 137
"Toscano, or Forbearance" ("Toscano, o la conformidad"), 74
Towns (Los pueblos), 19, 65, 66–70, 74, 92
Ultramarinos, 150n20
"vida de un español, La," *140n15*
"Woman, A" ("Una mujer"), 30
Baquero Goyanes, Mariano, 149n15
Barja, César, 140n11
Baroja, Pío, 17, 18, 21, 33, 37, 38, 39, 41, 85, 87; *Tree of Knowledge, The*, 87–88; *Way to Perfection, The*, 18, 37
Bécquer, Gustavo Adolfo, 85, 93

Bellas Artes, 16
Benavente, Jacinto, 17
Berceo, Gonzalo de, 17, 55, 70, 84, 92–93; *Miracles of Our Lady*, 92
Berkeley, George, 129
Bernard, Jean–Jacques, 148n2
Bernini, 98
Biervliet d'Overbroeck, M. D. van, 143n11, 147n21, 152n32
Bishop, Thomas, 148n2
Blanco Aguinaga, Carlos, 141n2, 144–45n2
Blanco y Negro, 76, 146n13
Blasco Ibáñez, Vicente, 114, 152–53n2
Booth, Wayne C., 145n9

Cadalso, José, 85, 87, 89
Calderón de la Barca, Pedro, 85, 91, 110, 124, 154n16; *gran teatro del mundo, El*, 154n16; *Life Is a Dream*, 91, 110, 124, 125
Compoamor, Ramón de, 85
Castro, Guillén de, 81
Castro, Rosalía de, 85, 86, 90
Catena de Vindel, Elena, 143n19
Celestina, 23, 33, 78, 84
Cervantes, Miguel de, 13, 21, 51, 71, 72, 73, 75, 78, 82, 83, 84, 90, 93, 111, 151n28; *coloquio de los perros, El*, 151n28; *Don Quixote*, 15–16, 33, 69, 70, 71, 72, 73, 82, 84, 88, 90, 93, 111, 125, 154n12; *Illustrious Kitchen Maid, The*, 75, 78; *Man of Glass, The*, 51; *Persiles and Sigismunda*, 93
Charles II, 32
Charles III, 27
Charrière, Isabelle de, 97
Clarín. See Alas, Leopoldo
Clavería, Carlos, 141n23
Coleridge, Samuel Taylor, 126
Constant, Benjamin, 96, 97, 100
Costa, Joaquín, 87

Delicado, Francisco, 75; *Exuberant Andalusian, The*, 75
Denner, Heinrich, 140n18
Descartes, René, 129
Díaz-Plaja, Guillermo, 152n35
Dicenta, Joaquín, 29
Doménech, Ricardo, 152n35

Durán, Agustín, 89

Echegaray, José, 85
Einstein, Albert, 94
Enguídanos, Miguel, 143n19
Espadas, Elizabeth, 140n18
España, 18, 19, 145n7, 145n12
Espronceda, José de, 85
Evreinov, Nikolai, 94

Feijóo, Benito Jerónimo, 85
Ferdinand the Catholic, 31
Fernández de Moratín, Leandro, 26, 85, 88
Fiddian, R.W., 142n4
Flaubert, Gustave, 28, 119
Ford, Richard, 77; *Handbook for Travellers in Spain*, 77
Fox, E. Inman, 139n9, 141n2, 142ch3n8, 143nn11-12, 146n20, 147nn23-24, 152n35
Frank, Joseph, 155n23
Freud, Sigmund, 94

Gantillon, Simon, 94, 148n2
Garcilaso de la Vega, 24, 81, 82, 84
Gautier, Théophile, 88, 139n4
Ghirlandaio, 47
Gillet, Joseph E., 151n24
Goethe, Johann Wolfgang von, 91
Gómez de la Serna, Ramón, 144n1
Góngora, Luis de, 17, 22, 81, 85, 86
Goytisolo, Luis, 155n2; *verdes de mayo hasta el mar, Los*, 155n2
Gracián, Baltasar, 75, 85, 86, 87, 88, 89, 154n19; *criticón, El*, 154n19; *Oráculo manual y arte de prudencia*, 154n19
Granada, Fray Luis de, 84
Granell, Manuel, 141n23, 148n3, 154n17
Grau, Jacinto, 109
Greco, El, 17, 22, 35, 78, 82
Gregory I, 27
Guillén, Jorge, 86, 150n20
Guinda Urzanqui, Julia (wife), 19–20, 21, 52, 119
Guyau, Jean Marie, 142ch3n5

Hamon, Augustin, 27, 28; "On the Fatherland," 28

Hoffmann, E. T. A., 60

Imparcial, El, 18, 19, 49, 70
Isabella the Catholic, 31, 75
Isla, Padre José Francisco de, 85

Jiménez, Juan Ramón, 86
Joiner, Lawrence D., 144n21, 155n26
Jovellanos, Gaspar Melchor de, 85
Juan de la Cruz, San, 84
Juan Manuel, Don, 84, 91; *Count Lucanor*, 91
Juventud, 17

Kant, Immanuel, 142ch3n5
Kattan, Olga, 152n35
Krause, Anna, 140n11, 140n13, 142ch3n6, 144n25, 145n6
Kropotkin, Peter, 28; "Prisons," 28

Laín Entralgo, Pedro, 139n5, 140–41n21
LaJohn, Lawrence Anthony, 152n35
Larra, Mariano José de, 17, 18, 27, 29, 30, 38, 85, 86, 87, 88, 89, 140n11, 144n25, 145n12; "All Souls' Day, 1836," 27; *doncel de don Enrique el Doliente, El*, 144n25; "I Want to Be an Actor," 30; *Macías*, 144n25; "Vuelva usted mañana," 145n12
Lazarillo de Tormes, 69, 75, 78, 82, 84, 86, 124
Lemaître, Georges, 149n7
Lenormand, Henri-René, 148n2
León, Fray Luis de, 80, 81, 84
Litvak, Lily, 145n8
Livingstone, Leon, 35, 102, 136, 139n10, 140n18, 141n23, 143n19, 147n26, 149–50n18, 151n24, 152n33, 153n3, 154n10, 154n18, 154n21, 155n24
Lott, Robert E., 148–49n4, 149n7, 149n11, 149n13–15, 151n26, 151n29, 152n35, 154n17, 154n19
Lucian, 124, 154n19; *True History*, 154n19

Machado, Antonio, 17, 86, 90, 146n18; "A José María Palacio," 146n18; *Fields of Castile*, 90

Macías el Enamorado, 63, 144n25
Madariaga, Pilar de, 154n12
Maeterlinck, Maurice, 28, 152n34; *Intruder, The*, 28
Maeztu, Ramiro de, 17, 18
Mainer, José Carlos, 154n13
Malón de Chaide, Pedro, 153n7
Manrique, Jorge, 84
Maragall, Juan, 81
Maravall, José Antonio, 141n23
March, Ausias, 114
Marco Merenciano, Francisco, 153–54n10
Marías, Julián, 143n19
Martínez, Isidro (father), 14
Martínez Cachero, José María, 143n18, 153n3
Martínez de Pisón, Eduardo, 146n14
Maura, Antonio, 19, 140n13
Maurois, André, 139n2
Meehan, Thomas C., 143n19
Meléndez Valdés, Juan, 85, 86
Menéndez y Pelayo, Marcelino, 91, 147n22
Mercantil Valenciano, El, 16
Meredith, George, 91
Mesonero Romanos, Ramón de, 88
Miró, Gabriel, 85
Montaigne, Michel Eyquem de, 46, 67; *Essays*, 67
Montes Huidobro, Matías, 143n19
Moratín. See Fernández de Moratín, Leandro
Mor de Fuentes, José, 85, 86, 87
Morris, C. B., 149n7
Muñoz Seca, Pedro, 94, 152n35; *Clamor, El*, 152n35

Nakens, José, 31
Newberry, Wilma, 152n35
Nietzsche, Friedrich, 45, 49, 67, 123, 139n4, 142ch3n5
Noel, Eugenio, 146n16
Núñez de Arce, Gaspar, 85

Ortega Munilla, José, 70
Ortega y Gasset, José, 140n19, 141n22, 146n20, 148n1; *deshumanización del arte e ideas sobre la novela, La*, 148n1
Ovid, 79, 81

País, El, 28, 29
Palley, Julian, 143n19
Pantoja de la Cruz, Juan, 75
Pardo Bazán, Emilia, 26, 85
Pellerin, Jean-Victor, 148n2
Pereda, José María de, 85
Pérez Galdós, Benito, 82, 85, 87, 147n23; *Electra*, 147n23
Pérez López, Manuel María, 145n3, 147n24
Philip II, 46, 71
Pirandello, Luigi, 94, 154n12; *Così è (se vi pare)*, 154n12
Pi y Margall, Francisco, 142ch3n6
Plato, 27
Poem of the Cid, 81–82, 84, 90, 92
Prensa, La (Buenos Aires), 20, 150n20
Pueblo, El, 16, 114

Quevedo, Francisco de, 85, 91, 93, 125, 148n30

Ramsden, H., 145n11
Rand, Marguerite C., 143n14, 148n28
Raphael, 47
Récamier, Julie, 97, 98, 99, 150n19
Reig, Carola, 148n28
Rembrandt, 154n15
Revista Nueva, 17
Rico Verdú, José, 143n9
Ridruejo, Dionisio, 153n3
Rilke, Rainer Maria, 149n11, 150n20, 152n34; *Notebooks of Malte Laurids Brigge, The*, 152n34
Risco, Antonio, 155n2
Rivas, Duque de, 85
Roderick, 21
Roh, Franz, 154n17
Rousseau, Jean Jacques, 128
Royal Spanish Academy, 21, 27, 65, 94
Rozas, Juan Manuel, 77, 146n15
Ruiz, Juan, 17, 70, 84
Ruiz, María Luisa (mother), 14–15
Ruiz de Alarcón, Juan, 85

Saavedra Fajardo, Diego de, 85, 86–87, 89
Sáinz de Bujanda, Fernando, 139n9, 147n21
Salinas, Pedro, 86, 150n20

Santillana, Marqués de, 17, 84
Schopenhauer, Arthur, 40, 45, 67, 142ch3n5
Seeleman, Rosa, 148n28
Servodidio, Mirella d'Ambrosio, 149n15
Shakespeare, William, 27
Shelley, Percy Bysshe, 127; "To a Sky-lark," 127
Sobejano, Gonzalo, 139n4, 143n15
Socrates, 27
Somoza, José, 93
Sophocles, 110; Oedipus at Colonus, 110
Staël, Madame de, 97
Stimson, Frederick S., 152n34
Stirner, Max, 45

Teresa de Jesús, Santa, 35, 84, 88, 97, 98, 99, 100, 102, 103, 123, 150n19
Tirso de Molina, 85
Torrente Ballester, Gonzalo, 155n2; Fragmentos de apocalipsis, 155n2
Torres Villarroel, Diego de, 85
Turner, Joseph Mallord William, 128; Evening Star, The, 128

Unamuno, Miguel de, 17, 19, 37, 109, 141n21, 151n24; Love and Pedagogy, 37; Niebla, 151n24

Valera, Juan, 85, 147n25
Valle-Inclán, Ramón María del, 17, 37, 109; Autumn Sonata, 37
Valverde, José María, 139n7, 140n14, 141n1, 143n11, 153n2
Vega, Lope de, 73, 85, 88
Velázquez, Diego, 74, 75; Meninas, Las, 74, 80
Verlaine, Paul, 139n4
Vermeer, 52
Verne, Jules, 15
Vidal, José B., 143n19
Virgil, 81
Vives, Juan Luis, 84, 114
Voltaire, 19

Zdenek, Joseph W., 155n26
Zorrilla, José, 58, 63; Don Juan Tenorio, 58
Zuloaga, Ignacio, 136

DATE DUE